COOKING KETO WITH KRISTIE

JOURNEY TO HEALTH:
A Journey Worth Taking

Kristie H. Sullivan, Ph.D.

Journey to Health: A Journey Worth Taking

DEDICATION

This book is dedicated to my sweet family—David, Grace, and Jonathan who love me enough to let me pursue this effort. They are my taste testers, my most vocal critics, and my strongest allies, and also to my mom who always told me I could.

This book is also dedicated to those who endeavor to make a ketogenic diet a lifelong commitment to better health. Thank you for sharing this journey with me.

Journey to Health: A Journey Worth Taking

ACKNOWLEDGMENTS

My sincerest gratitude and appreciation for the direct help and support given to me
by the following people:

Robin Rourke, without whom this book would not have happened

My focus group who patiently reassured me and reviewed no fewer than two dozen covers
and listened to all of my insecurities for months:

*Kristen Duckett, Debbie Roach, Sandy Amaya, Willow Thomason, Bill Croft,
Paula Wisor, Laurie Lyon, Bill Barrons, Laurie Bizzell, Shannon Worgan,
Colon Mills, Carol Gonzalez, and Barb Sims*

My sweet supporters who tested recipes and took photographs. Even if I wasn't able to use their photos, I am
especially grateful for the generous giving of their time and enthusiasm to see this book completed:

*Debbie Roach, Sondy Murray, Crystal Pullen, Krik Pullen Photography, Rebecca Scavello,
Kimberley Tosello, Susan Hopp-Johnson, Sue Guzman, Kim Hardie, Kit Schroder, Lori Weed,
Carol Pitts, Jan Walinck, Robyn Marquez, Kat Macie, Brenda Atkins Westman Kukla,
Danita Blevins, Whitney Blevins, Sandy Amaya and Jen Reitz Scholz*

A special thank you to my dear friend *Maggie Bonecutter* who was the first to say the magical words,
"It isn't always about the calories."

And now a note from my attorney…..

This is a cookbook for those who have decided to follow a very low carb or ketogenic lifestyle. This book offers no medical claims, no health claims, or nutritional advice.

Every reasonable effort has been made to ensure the accuracy of the information contained in this book; however, it is possible that mistakes were overlooked and as such the reader must independently confirm any information on which reliance is needed. As such, the author and publisher make no warranties about the contents of the book, except that the author and her family have enjoyed eating their way through each recipe.

TABLE OF CONTENTS

TABLE OF CONTENTS

TABLE OF CONTENTS

1 WHY THIS BOOK?

Following a ketogenic diet for me began as a desperate way to lose weight. I was forty-five years old, morbidly obese, and in constant pain from back issues. My children were young, and I couldn't do things for them or with them that I wanted to do. My back pain was so severe in the evenings that it was very difficult for me to walk. After dinner, I spent most evenings in bed. It was difficult to climb the stairs to tuck them into bed, so most nights they came into my bedroom, kissed me, and went up to their own beds. On trips, David and the children would go for a walk or a hike as I waited in the car or the hotel alone. Even though I had a professional job that I enjoyed, married a fantastic husband, had two amazing kids, a nice house, and more material possessions than we needed, my quality of life was not very good. Because of the obesity and back issues, I wasn't the wife or mother that I wanted to be. I was convinced that my family was cheated from what they deserved, and that they deserved far more than what I could offer.

My family at Disney World in October 2008. Five years before I discovered a ketogenic diet.

Losing weight and keeping the weight off had been a lifetime struggle. I became obese around the age of three. When I think of my childhood, I remember being hungry—always hungry and sneaking food from the kitchen and hoping I wouldn't get caught. Store bought clothes wouldn't fit me, so my mother and grandmother sewed many of my clothes. I dieted off and on, restricting calories, walking, and promising that I'd "start that diet tomorrow after I finished off the cookies, cake, and chocolate." So many tomorrows brought that same promise. There were a few exceptions. In my sophomore year of college I starved myself to a size 16 until I could starve no more and then binged my way back up to a size 22. In my senior year of college, I joined a physician's-assisted weight loss clinic, ate low fat and low carb and exercised every day and lost down to a size 14 before giving up that misery.

By the time I was 28, I weighed 313 pounds and had a hard time finding clothing in a size 26. I had completed a master's degree and bought my first house, but could not control my weight. Gastric bypass surgery seemed like a good idea then. In 1997, gastric bypass was still relatively new, but I was determined and desperate. I chose to have surgery at a medical school that was a three hour drive from my home. Not only was there no real follow-up, but the doctors and nutritionists in my rural area had no idea how to provide follow-up care for bariatric patients, and I was too thrilled to have lost weight to worry about nutritional deficiencies or changing my eating patterns. I had gone from weighing 313 lbs to 178 lbs. when I joined a gym that provided nutritional counseling as part of my membership. A hospital-affiliated nutritionist was aghast at my eating journal. She told me that I needed to eat more carbs, so two years post-op, I added carbohydrates and promptly began gaining weight. From 2000 to 2013 I tried to follow a low fat, low calorie diet. I joined Weight Watchers at least three or four times and discussed weight loss medications with my doctors. My gynecologist encouraged me to have the gastric bypass surgery revised so that I could lose more weight when her scales showed I'd tipped over 250 lbs. By then I had two children, was finishing my Ph.D., and had a very demanding job.

So I found myself in May 2013 weighing over 250 lbs, having constant debilitating back pain, and missing out on much of life. I had done most of what I'd ever wanted to do. As a single woman, I had bought a house on my own, later met and married the love of my life, had two children in spite of multiple miscarriages and pregnancy complications and difficult births that made each of their survivals small miracles. I had completed advanced degrees and established a career in which I was respected by others in the field. By many measures my life was a success, but I felt like a complete failure. How could I have accomplished so many difficult things, yet never conquered my weight? Why was I considered really smart, but too dumb to figure out how to manage my diet? I knew something was missing, but the only thing offered by my doctor was low fat, caloric restriction and appetite suppressants. I decided to knuckle down one last time. With clenched teeth, I made an oath to lose the weight or die trying. I was serious about that. If I couldn't be the wife and mother that my family deserved, than I thought they would be better off without me.

My kids were young, and I hated that could not keep up with them.

Armed with resolve of steel, I began a strict 1200 calorie diet. For two weeks I logged every morsel of food I ate. I went to the gym, where I climbed stairs and treaded on treadmills and sweated, which I hate to do. The first week, I lost weight. I was hungry and miserable, but I lost weight, so it seemed worth it. The second week I lost nothing. Not an ounce. I had logged all of my food and eaten hardly anything at all except low fat foods, and I had gotten headaches and hangry, and I had not lost a pound. My heart sank. What if I couldn't do this? What if I simply could not lose weight? I wanted to succeed, but I obviously didn't know how. Lost, I remembered that Maggie, a friend from church had shared that she had been overweight as a child, but had lost weight. I wondered if she might be able to share a secret, so I called her and described the previous two weeks of misery, and she said, "It isn't always about the calories." I had never heard that before. She told me about a book by a man named Gary Taubes, Why We Get Fat and What to do About It. June 19, 2013 I ordered the book that would change my life. Amazon sent me that book in two days. I read it in two days and told my husband that I was going to follow the eating plan by Dr. Eric Westman from Duke University who had a short eating guide in the Appendix of Taubes' book. David looked over my shoulder as I pointed a stubby finger at the what not to eat section. I read, "No sugar, no starch, no potatoes, no rice." David said, "No way!" He smiled down at me in a most condescending way and said, "Good luck with that. Let me know how it goes." The man who had watched weight with me and counted points and grilled chicken and washed the dishes and tucked the babies in and helped me walk in the evenings was drawing a line in the sand. And why shouldn't he? I'd tried some ridiculous diet stuff before. No need for him to get too worked up. In his mind, I might try that diet for a day or two and then I would be on to the next crazy thing while we ate doughnuts and complained about being fat.

His apathy didn't deter me because as I had read Taubes' book, it resonated with me. What Taubes described had been true for me. The insatiable hunger had followed me all the days of my life, and it wasn't because there was something wrong with me. There was something wrong with what I was eating. If Taubes was right, and if this no sugar, no starch plan from this doctor at Duke worked as Taubes described, then my body would know. What had become abundantly clear from my friend and from Taubes' book was that this "diet" only worked if you followed it 100%. If you ate sugar and starch even a little bit, and blood glucose rose, then you would raise insulin and insulin is a hoarder hormone that shoves fat into cells and keeps it locked there like little soldier meanie-guys. The goal, as I understood it, was to keep blood glucose stable, lower levels of insulin and unlock stored fat. Taubes had described obesity as a state of starving because the stored energy was unable to be released.

Kristie NOT cooking keto in 2011. I was making homemade sour dough bread, using low fat ingredients, canola oil, and a "healthy" buttery spread.

I didn't study the eating plan for two weeks. I didn't make a special shopping trip. I didn't read four more books or Google any more information. I started eating low carb high fat the very next day. For dinner, I made a traditional meal of a meat and two vegetables, but I made sure one side was low carb for me. By day two I noticed that I wasn't all that hungry. On day three, it was late afternoon when I realized I'd actually forgotten to eat lunch. While that might not be a big deal for some people, I was that person who had previously kept a drawer full of snacks. My office was better stocked than any vending machine. Of course, I had "healthy" granola bars, candy, peanut butter crackers, and low fat cookies. My normal eating pattern used to be breakfast, snack, lunch, snack, dinner, snack, bed, and that was on days when I wasn't hungry. Because of hypoglycemia, I kept food with me at all times — in the office, in my purse, and in my car. When I had gone from 7:00 am to 3:00 pm without thinking about food, I knew that I was on to something different.

For two weeks I ate low carb high fat while my family ate what I ate, but also ate whatever carbs they wanted. My husband still drank Pepsi, and the family ate bread and potatoes. I kept my carbs to under 20 total grams per day. During that time I didn't exercise. I wasn't hangry, and I didn't feel deprived until the end of the second week when I had an unnatural craving for a chocolate chip cookie. It took all of my resolve to avoid driving straight to the grocery store and buying not one, but two bags of Pepperidge Farm soft baked cookies. I even imagined myself doing it. I'm not sure what stopped me except that I knew that giving in would negate all of my progress. Before I started, I had promised myself two weeks of a solid try. I never promised that I would never eat another chocolate chip cookie, but I told myself that I would follow that doctor's plan for two weeks just to see it if worked. In the meantime, I was desperate for a cookie. That's when I did a Google search and found a simple four-ingredient peanut butter cookie. I had all four ingredients in my cabinets. As I made those cookies I worried that eating them would interfere with my progress. I promised myself that I would eat only two cookies. Just two. I stood in the kitchen savoring those two warm cookies and thought, almost out loud, "If I can eat this and still lose weight, then I can do this for the rest of my life." The scales were down a pound the next day, and I haven't stopped keto.

So why this book? Even though my husband and I have been on a ketogenic diet since June 2013, our family physician still asks whether this "diet" is sustainable. In fact, more than one medical professional has told me that this way of eating is "too difficult to follow" or "too restrictive". Even those who have told me that this is a great way to eat, have also told me that it's too hard. Some say they don't ask their patients to follow it because of difficulties with compliance. I spend a lot of time thinking about why this way of eating is hard for some people. My desperate plan to lose weight evolved after I started the journey, and eventually this way of eating became a way to manage my health and not just my weight. While I enjoy eating the best foods of my life and losing weight, I also have come to appreciate that my overall health has improved. I no longer need any of the four medications that I was on before I started keto. I no longer wait in the car or at the hotel while my family hikes. Now I'm the one who suggests that we go for walk or go kayaking or play at the pool. There are days when I still fall short of being the mother or wife I'd like to be, but it is no longer because of the obesity.

When I try to understand why it might difficult for others to transition to a ketogenic lifestyle, then I focus on why it seemed to work for me.

Spring 2015. The first time we ever had professional photographs taken of the entire family except for the church directory.

• I was desperate. I would have given up another organ to lose weight. I would have taken any drug, supplement, or medication offered to me. To "give up" sugar and starch seemed inconsequential to me. Sure, I loved those high carbohydrate foods, but I hated being obese more. That misery and resolve provided powerful motivation.

• I focused on the foods that I could eat. From the manual by Dr. Westman, I read the food lists over and over again. That booklet was by my side at work, in the car, and at home. If I was in the kitchen, the book was in the kitchen. When I went to bed at night, I had the book by my nightstand. This was the first diet that told me I could eat steak and bacon and hamburgers. When I ate those foods, my body was satisfied. The hunger was quiet, and I was grateful. When you are satisfied, you do not miss the sugar and starches because nothing is missing. By focusing on the foods that I could eat and that I enjoyed, I also created new food habits. Instead of wishing for chocolate chip cookies, I made my own low carb versions.

• I felt better. Right away I noticed that not only was I not hungry, but I felt better. I felt lighter. My scales chronicled the progress, and my clothes were looser. Success breeds success, and I was encouraged and motivated by seeing the progress. My focus shifted from weight loss to improving my health, and as my health improved I no longer needed daily anti-inflammatory medications or pain medications for my back.

• I understood that my body is carbohydrate intolerant. Phinney and Volek discuss this in their book The Art and Science of Low Carbohydrate Living. In a way similar to someone with a peanut allergy, my body simply cannot process carbohydrates efficiently. Instead of using carbohydrates for energy, my body becomes sick. Obesity, for me, was a symptom of that intolerance. Obesity was never the disease, but a symptom of the underlying inflammation. Managing the inflammation by eating fewer carbohydrates allows me to remain healthy. That simple concept makes it far easier for me to reject high carb foods and to consistently make healthier choices for my body. Seeing a high carb cake or bread or side dish doesn't appeal to me simply

My first piggy-back ride since I was six-years old, and I love that David can pick me up!

because I see that as food that my body doesn't tolerate. Those foods might taste good temporarily, but ultimately, they make me sick. Knowing that gives me the fortitude to avoid any temptation to eat off plan.

• Just for today. More than anything, I committed to this way of eating for two weeks and was determined to see if it "worked". Each time I was tempted to eat off plan, I remembered why I started. I remembered the clothes I couldn't wear, the things I couldn't do. Each day I used affirmations and promised "Just for today, I choose me". Each day that I chose me, I woke up feeling stronger and less hungry and happier and healthier. When my two-week commitment was over, I knew that this was exactly what my body needed. This cookbook has the recipes that made me successful. It is my most sincere hope that they help you too.

You can learn more about my own journey to health and follow my latest updates at www.cookingketowithkristie.com. You can also follow my Facebook page, Simply Keto and subscribe to my YouTube channel, Cooking Keto with Kristie.

2 USING ALTERNATIVE INGREDIENTS

As someone who cooks by smell, taste, and feel it wasn't easy for me to learn how to cook low carb high fat. I was especially challenged when it came to using alternative flours and oils in baking. While using traditional flours was somewhat intuitive, using nut flours or coconut flour was not. For the first six to nine months on keto, I followed low carb recipes to the letter—something I had rarely done! Slowly I gained some confidence and took a few risks and learned some hard lessons. If you've ever wondered what ingredients to use in low carb baked goods or why an ingredient is used or what ingredients combine well with others, then this information might be helpful. Also, if you've ever found a recipe that looks and sounds fantastic, but you're missing an obscure ingredient and you've wondered if you could make a substitution so that you don't have to buy more strange ingredients that seem available only online, then this information may be helpful.

Alternative flours. What helps texture and what adds bulk or substance?

• **Almond flour.** Although it can be pricey, it's a good standard nut flour. It also burns easily, so if you're baking with it, keep the oven temperature at 350 degrees or lower. Another advantage is dense and heavy and needs to be paired with other flours or agents that provide some volume or rise. Almond flour doesn't absorb moisture like other more "thirsty" options. It's versatile and a good staple to keep on hand for a keto kitchen. You can use it in cookies, brownies, cakes, biscuits, breads, muffins, pie crusts, etc. It's generally available at Wal-Mart, Costco, Trader Joe's, Aldi's, Big Lots, Sam's Club, and local grocers. Please know that almond meal is thicker and more coarse and will result in a more dense baked good than a finer almond flour (which I prefer). You can also buy almond flour online at Honeyville (my favorite), Netrition, or Amazon.

• **Coconut flour.** Another great staple to keep on hand. It plays well with almond flour, but it isn't as easygoing. The qualities of coconut flour can vary somewhat by brand and can be impacted by humidity in storage which can also affect baking results. Coconut flour is "thirsty" and needs more liquid as well as additional eggs to provide structure. For all of its finickiness, it gives a great texture to low carb baked goods. It results in a lighter texture and finer crumb than almond flour. Unlike almond flour, a little goes a long way. Two tablespoons of coconut flour combined with a cup or a cup and a half of almond flour is a common base used in a lot of low carb baked goods. Coconut flour retains a gritty consistency. It cannot be used as a creamy thickener for soups, casseroles, or gravies; however, it is wonderful in cookies, brownies, cakes, muffins, pie crusts, etc. Coconut flour is typically paired with almond flour or another nut flour to give it bulk and to lower carbohydrates. It can be found in some local grocers or national chains. It also is available at the online stores I listed above for almond flour.

• **Pork rinds.** You thought those were just for snacks or nachos or dipping in guacamole? Or maybe you've wrinkled your nose in disdain for them when you brushed by them in the gas station. Either way, if you're not cooking with them, you're missing out! I have a YouTube video dedicated to my love of pork rinds and many of the useful ways you can use them. https://www.youtube.com/watch?v=mQqpTiVlEwg

When finely crushed, pork rinds make a great flour. They can be used in sweet or savory dishes, and are surprisingly flavor neutral for the most part as long as you buy unflavored and stick to the fluffier skins rather than the crunchier cracklin' versions. I have used pork rind dust in pancakes, casseroles, and as breading for chicken, fish, and country style steak. Pork rinds provide a gelatinous texture and are slightly thirsty. They are good for texture. Most grocery stores have them, but my favorite place to buy them is convenience stores in rural areas. I've discovered my favorite brands by stopping at independently owned service stations in the middle of nowhere. No, I'm not obsessed. Why do you ask?

• **Hazelnut, walnut, pecan flour.** These behave much like almond flour in terms of providing volume, but they are also more dense and heavy, but not "thirsty" like coconut flour. They can generally be easily interchanged with almond flour in recipes. They have a stronger flavor profile especially when you pair them with their corresponding nut oil. For example, hazelnut pairs well with chocolate for a "Nutella" flavor. Using hazelnut oil in the batter enhances the subtle flavor. The same is true for walnuts. These flours are not as easy to find in local stores or national grocers, but can be ordered online from the websites I mentioned as sources for almond flour. Hazelnut is lower in carbs than almond flour, and I enjoy using it in baked goods.

• **Nut butters.** These can be used for making cookies, brownies, fudge, or "fat bombs". Nut butters are thick and dense. You can make your own from grinding nuts or you can buy them. While not a staple in baking, the very first low carb treat I ever made was a very simple recipe that used 1 cup of peanut butter, 1 cup of granulated sweetener, 1 egg, 1 tsp vanilla, 1/4 tsp salt. Mix all of that, scoop batter into cookies, and place onto a piece of parchment paper on a baking sheet. Bake at 350 degrees for 9-12 minutes. Don't overbake and don't burn your mouth trying to eat them straight from the oven! These are the cookies literally saved my life by keeping me on plan. I remember thinking, "If I can eat these and lose weight, I can do this!" (recipe on page 135)

• **Oat fiber.** Yes, I have a little bit of a crush on this obscure ingredient. It is pure, insoluble fiber, and it does not impact blood glucose. Please note that oat *fiber* is not the same as oat bran. Those are higher carb. You want oat *fiber*. Oat fiber gives baked goods a wonderful, flour-like taste and texture. It makes low carb treats so much more like the "real thing". As for texture, it's very thirsty and behaves similar to coconut flour but has a softer texture. But, and you knew there was a but, right? It is derived from a grain. While it is gluten free, it is often processed in facilities in which cross contamination can occur. Typically it is only available online, and some vendors do sell a gluten free version; however, not all brands are created equal. I have found that some brands are too strong. My personal favorite is Life Source, which you can buy at Amazon or Netrition. Trim Healthy Momma is another good brand and is certified gluten-free. Like coconut flour, oat fiber pairs well with other flours. If you don't have it or can't find it, coconut flour makes a good substitute. Use about half of the same amount of coconut flour for oat fiber. Some brands have a very strong flavor, and I don't recommend those (Honeyville, Anthony's, and NuNaturals are very strong). Life Source or Trim Healthy Momma brands are my favorite.

• **Psyllium fiber.** Yes, it's just what you're thinking, a common fiber supplement. You can find it not in the baking aisles, but near the pharmacy section. It's very thirsty and can also add a gelatinous texture. I use it to make a low carb flatbread that my daughter and I love! Made with olive oil, the flatbread is the closest thing to low carb pita bread that I've ever had. It's another good staple to have on hand.

Additions that add volume, rise, or texture.

• **Baking powder.** Look for baking powder that is aluminum free. Trader Joe's has a good brand. It's a common ingredient in most kitchens, so I won't say much about it other than 1 to 2 teaspoons is a pretty standard amount to use in baked goods. Too much baking powder can cause baked goods to sink as they cool.

• **Baking soda.** Unlike baking powder, baking soda needs an agent to activate it. An acid like vinegar or lemon juice is perfect. Generally you add baking soda to your dry ingredients and the acid gets added at the end of mixing, typically with the wet ingredients. If you're like me and you like to taste test the batter before baking, please know that baking soda can give batter an "odd" taste. Don't be discouraged. That odd flavor disappears in the chemical process of baking.

- **Gelatin.** Unflavored gelatin is great for providing some of the structure that is missing when you are baking with ingredients that don't have gluten. Grass-fed beef or porcine gelatin can be ordered online or buy unflavored gelatin in any grocer. Knox is a common brand. Be sure to get unflavored.

- **Xanthan gum.** What to say about this stuff. It can help texture in baked goods and is generally listed as "optional". I have used it and been grateful at times and have also used it and wished I hadn't. The line between just enough and too much is hard for me to find. It can give baked goods a gummy texture if overdone. I keep it on hand and try to err on the side of using too little. A small bag is about $10, but should last for more than a year.

- **Glucomannan.** Made from the root of the konjac is a soluble fiber that has been documented to have no impact on blood glucose. It is a water-soluble fiber and is an excellent thickening agent. Use sparingly since it tends to thicken more as it cools. Unlike xanthan gum, glucomannan does not become slimy. They can often be used interchangeably, and I prefer to use glucomannan rather than xanthan gum. Be sure to sprinkle it evenly into wet ingredients or mix well with other dry ingredients before adding liquids. If not, it may clump.

- **Eggs.** Egg whites help provide volume and texture. Before following a ketogenic diet, I dutifully avoided any recipe that called for egg whites. For some reason I was highly intimidated. Let me assure you that if you have a clean bowl and a hand mixer, you can whip egg whites. You don't want any oily residue on the bowl or the beaters, but other than that, just beat until the egg whites are stiff. Generally, you beat them long enough that you can turn the bowl upside down and see no movement from egg whites. Also, you will typically fold the whipped egg whites into batter if you aren't making meringue. Folding means you gently incorporate the egg whites into the batter. A rubber spatula works well for this, and you simply keep running the spatula around the sides of the bowl and then thru the middle. If you stir egg whites in too roughly, they will deflate and lose volume.

Fats.

- **Butter.** We all know butter makes it better, right? Butter is my absolutely favorite fat to use in baking. Salted or unsalted, butter just reigns supreme in my kitchen.

- **MCT oil.** As long as you need a liquid fat, this is another good option, but not a necessity. MCT is medium chain triglycerides. It's a good fat and stays liquid at cold temperatures, which makes it ideal for smoothies or iced coffees.

- **Ghee.** Clarified butter. It's a good option for folks who are dairy free, but want the taste of butter. Since the milk solids are removed when the butter is clarified most lactose intolerant folks can enjoy ghee. It works well for pan-frying since it doesn't burn as butter does.
- **Bacon fat.** For savory baked goods such as low carb biscuits, breads, rolls, etc. it's a fantastic option! I save my bacon fat from cooking bacon in the oven and pouring the drippings into a recycled pickle jar by the stove. Liquid gold!

- **Avocado oil.** An excellent option to use with apple cider vinegar or coconut vinegar as a simple salad dressing. Avocado oil is also excellent when used to make mayonnaise.

- **Coconut oil.** Another keto staple. If you're dairy free, coconut oil is a great option. It behaves similarly to butter in baked goods and can be used interchangeably. Refined or unrefined are the two most basic options. For people who don't like the taste of coconut, refined coconut oil has little to no coconut flavor. Some prefer unrefined coconut oil and report that it has additional health benefits. Since my family is sensitive to the taste of coconut oil, I tend to use the refined. It is a great dairy free option. I use it in baking, roasting vegetables and in making fat bombs.

Sweeteners.

There are so many opinions about which sweeteners are safe and which ones are not. For the purpose of explaining my preferences, I'll stick to describing their use by texture, form (liquid, powder, granulated, etc.) and intensity. Regardless of which sweetener you choose, please be mindful that each of us is impacted differently. If you are diabetic, please use your meter to monitor your blood glucose to see whether a sweetener affects you adversely. You can view my video to learn more about my experiences with many different low carb sweeteners on the market. http://bit.ly/KetoSweeteners

- **Liquid sweeteners.** Besides taste, the form sweeteners take can be important. Most liquid sweeteners are very intense with just a few drops providing the equivalent of 1/4 to 1/2 cup of sugar. The liquid sweeteners with which I am most familiar are liquid sucralose and liquid stevia. The intensity of liquid stevia seems greater than liquid sucralose and varies widely by brand. Start with just a drop or two of either and add only a drop at a time until the batter tastes sweet enough. Liquid sweeteners can usually be interchanged without getting different results.

- **Granulated sweeteners.** In addition to taste, these can add bulk. Bulk or substance is often an important contribution. Erythritol, xylitol, Splenda are examples of bulk sweeteners. Erythritol is lightly less sweet than xylitol or Splenda. I do not use Splenda as it has been bulked with maltodextrin which behaves like sugar in our bodies. It raises my blood glucose, but some people can use it without any ill effects. Pure sucralose and powdered stevia are other non-liquid options, but they do not provide the bulk or substance that the others add. When I need bulk, I'll often use some erythritol or xylitol and then add powdered pure sucralose or stevia (a small pinch at a time) to achieve the desired sweetness. If you're using stevia, look for brands with 90% or higher steviosides to avoid the bitter aftertaste that can be common in stevia products.

- **Powdered sweeteners.** Sometimes recipes call for powdered sweeteners. This can be important when you need a smooth texture as in a ganache, "buttercream" frosting, or sauce. If a recipe calls for powdered sweetener, simply run your preferred granulated sweetener through a blender, Ninja, Bullet, etc. Some folks have reported that a regular blender doesn't work as well for powdering sweetener and that they have purchased a cheap coffee grinder just for that purpose.

My preferred sweetener is a combination of the natural sweeteners erythritol and stevia made by a company called Sukrin. SukrinUSA has an excellent variety of sweetener options, and they are by far my favorite in terms of taste. While I am not fond of the aftertaste I experience from pure erythritol, I do not detect any aftertaste from their products. The carbivore friends and family who sample the treats I make really like them too. In fact, I use their products exclusively, so you will see their sweeteners listed in my recipes. Among my favorites in their product line are the following:

Sukrin is pure granulated erythritol. While it looks and tastes like sugar it is only about 75% as sweet as sugar. Sukrin:1 is a blend of erythritol and stevia. It measures cup for cup like sugar. Sukin + is also a blend of erythritol and stevia, but has a higher proportion of stevia than Sukrin :1 making it more than twice as sweet as sugar. For baking, I tend to use Sukin :1 or Sukrin + most frequently. Sukrin Melis, also called Icing Sugar, is a powdered sweetener that has the same texture as powdered sugar. Melis is perfect for making low carb buttercream, frostings, or glazes. Use it to avoid the grittiness of granulated sweetener. Last, is Sukrin Gold, their brown sugar substitute. Sukrin Gold is the darling of their sweetener options and is unrivaled as an alternative to brown sugar. Using it gives the rich aroma and flavor of traditional brown sugar. I use it every chance I get.

Not only are their products delicious, but SukrinUSA is also a generous company. They have offered me a discount code to give you a 5% discount off your order at www.SukrinUSA.com. The discount code is: ketocook

Liquids and additional fats.

• **Sour cream.** This is a great inexpensive low carb option. Be sure to buy the full-fat version and check the ingredients to make sure no food starches are added.

• **Crème fraiche.** My favorite dairy! Crème fraiche is similar to sour cream, but has a much higher percentage of fat, lower carb count, and moderate protein. It can be used in sweet or savory recipes, and I prefer it because of the nutritional profile.

• **Mascarpone.** Another dairy darling! Similar to cream cheese, but not as thick or tangy, mascarpone can also be used in sweet or savory applications. It has more fat and less protein than cream cheese. I like to mix it with crème fraiche as a substitute for yogurt.

• **Greek yogurt.** When a recipe calls for Greek yogurt I generally cringe because it can be extremely difficult to find full fat yogurt with no added sugars. When I do find it, it's expensive. Most of the time I simply use sour cream or crème fraiche instead.

• **Heavy cream.** If you've watched any of my videos, you've likely heard me explain that heavy cream has a higher fat content than heavy whipping cream. It's true and I prefer heavy cream. If you can't find heavy cream, heavy whipping cream is a fine substitute. It adds a rich and creamy texture to recipes. Like butter, it's my preferred ingredient.

• **Coconut milk.** A good dairy free option. Can be substituted for cream, but if you need more thickness use coconut cream. Coconut milk does add a slight coconut flavor, so keep that in mind. Also, be persnickety when choosing a brand of coconut milk or coconut cream. Companies are notorious for adding sugars, stabilizers, thickeners, and flavors. You don't want any of that. Native Forest or Arroy-D are my preferred brands. I order both online. Trader Joe's has also had a good low carb coconut milk.

- **Coconut cream.** Another good dairy free option. It can be whipped just like heavy cream. Always check the ingredients of the coconut cream you use. Often ingredients and nutritional information vary widely by brand. You can also get coconut cream from a can of coconut milk by leaving it unopened in the refrigerator overnight, cutting the top off the can, and skimming the thicker cream from the top. I generally discard the liquid left behind.

- **Almond milk.** Another dairy free option, but much thinner than heavy cream. Sometimes the thinner texture is exactly what you need. Just as with coconut milk and coconut cream, take care when purchasing almond milk. Food companies love to add sugars and thickeners and flavors. You want the ingredient list to be very simple — almond milk.

Obviously, those are just the basics, and I've likely omitted someone's favorite ingredient, but I wanted to share just an overview of some of the tips and tricks I've picked up over the time that I've been cooking keto. You can also watch me discuss using alterative ingredients on my YouTube channel, Cooking Keto with Kristie. In this video I give a very basic review of what ingredients I keep on hand and how I combine alternative ingredients to make low carb recipes.
http://bit.ly/AlternativeIngredients

Important Notes:

Nutritional Information

While I have provided nutritional information for each recipe, please understand that the information I provide is based on the carb counts for the ingredients that I use. Ingredients can vary widely. For example, cream cheese varies from one total carb per serving to two per one ounce serving. Because I use only the brands of cream cheese that have 1 total carb per ounce, when a recipe calls for 8 ounces of cream cheese, I count that as 8 total carbs in the nutritional count. Please keep in mind that you should count it as 16 total carbs if you are using a different cream cheese. While working on the nutritional information for this book I noticed that different brands of chorizo, sausage, tomato sauce, mascarpone, coconut milk, and other foods were likely to have widely varying nutritional information. Please use the nutritional information that I provide as a guide; however, it is not intended to be a substitute for calculating your own nutritional information based serving sizes and the ingredients you use.

In addition, I do not count sugar alcohols for erythritol as it does not raise blood glucose for most people; however, if you are diabetic, please test to know whether it affects you. Also, I do not count the carbohydrates in oat fiber because it is pure, insoluble fiber that passes through the body completely unabsorbed. Again, I encourage you to calculate the macronutrients for each ingredient you use. There are several good online recipe calculators that allow you to select the brands that you use.

Baking Times

One of my most treasured possessions from my grandmother are her handwritten recipes. She jotted them down on scraps of paper, listing each ingredient and then providing written directions for the preparation. Nearly all of her baked goods ended with "Bake until done." Yes. Bake until done. No baking times or guidelines such as "until center is set". Due to variations in ingredients, oven temperatures, pan sizes, altitude, etc. baking times may vary from my house to yours For these reasons, for baked items, I tried to offer a range of baking times as well as guidelines for how the finished product should look or feel.

Substitutions

Where possible, I have tried to suggest substitutions. In most cases your preferred granulated or liquid sweetener may be used. You may want to add less sweetener so that you can more easily adjust it to your tastes. Also, some people have difficulty finding oat fiber. I have suggested how to substitute coconut flour in most of the recipes. With some exceptions, you should use half the amount of coconut flour for oat fiber. Therefore, if a recipe calls for 1/4 cup of oat fiber, simply use 2 tablespoons of coconut flour. Last, xanthan gum can generally be substituted for glucomannan or omitted from most baked goods.

Now…let's cook keto!!

Chapter 1
RISE & SHINE

Breakfast options become so much easier when you let go of the notion of traditional breakfast foods. More than once, I've heard someone lament that they are sick of bacon and eggs. Let's be clear. I rarely eat bacon and eggs for breakfast. Breakfast is literally to "break a fast". Think of it as your first meal of the day and not as a meal that has to include eggs, bagels, toasts, bacon, sausage, etc. My favorite breakfast is a fatty hamburger with bacon and cheese. For a real treat serve it with a fried sunny-side up egg. When you break the yolk, the rich fatty goodness is absorbed into the beef and just sings "Good morning!" to you! I've also been known to eat bacon and pimento cheese or sausage with cream cheese. Simple, low carb goodness that keeps me from hunger for at least 4 to 6 hours is the most important criteria I look for in a breakfast meal. The second most important criteria is that it is quick. I either need to be able to make it ahead of time or make it quickly as we all scurry out the door for work and school.

In this section I have included some of my favorite low carb breakfast foods. All are low carb versions of traditional breakfasts. Here's a confession. None of us in my family really love eggs, so all of the breakfast recipes here that use eggs, relegate them to the sidelines instead of center field. My versions of frittatas are created for people who really don't like eggs, so they have enough fat and protein to hide the egg flavor. I've include three variations of frittatas or crustless egg casseroles that are hearty and easy to make ahead of time for those of us on the go. I've served these to carbivores for brunches and everyone always asks for the recipe. There are also recipes for traditional southern favorites like sausage gravy and creamed chip beef — can you believe those are part of a "diet' book? Serve those over one of my biscuit recipes or over toasted soul bread and you will never feel deprived again. There's even a recipe for a breakfast pizza that works well to share or make ahead of time so that your family can warm a slice easily. For those of you who enjoy yogurt, there's "faux-gurt". In spite of it being touted as "healthy", a good high fat and low sugar yogurt is hard to find, so I've included my favorite substitutes that won't throw you off plan. Last, in the savory category is a breakfast bomb. Like a fat bomb, these are full of fat and protein and very low carb. They are easy to make ahead of time, travel well, but are delicious enough to add to a brunch buffet and serve to guests although you might want to name them something different to make them more appealing to others.

If sweeter options such as pancakes, waffles, or muffins are your ideal breakfast, you can still have low carb options. I've included two types of pancakes. One of them uses crushed pork rinds. Don't worry. Even those who don't like the taste of pork rinds have enjoyed them used as a flour substitute in pancakes. If you don't tell them, your family and friends could never imagine that you've used pork rinds to make pancakes. You will be equally surprised at the blueberry cream cheese muffin recipe. More than one person has told me that they taste just like a high carb version. This is a versatile, basic recipe, and I include ideas for variations using it. If you like sweet breads, there's also a recipe for apple spice bread that can be made as a muffin or as a loaf. It doesn't use apples because those are too high carb, but if you follow the recipe, you won't miss the apples, or the glucose spike, at all. Last, the chapter concludes with two options for coffee, including a pumpkin spice flavor and a hazelnut coffee creamer. These are included because many low carbers enjoy coffee with butter for breakfast, and there are times when all of us want a little guiltless guilty pleasure with our coffee.

Country Ham, Cheese, & Broccoli Frittata

This is my favorite flavor of frittata. The country ham reminds me of my grandmother who always reserved country ham for a special occasion, like Sunday morning! In this dish, the country ham bakes up tender and adds just a hint of salt. The broccoli gives a little texture, and the cheese makes it creamy and rich.
Video: http://bit.ly/CookingKetoWithKristieFrittata

INGREDIENTS

8 eggs
1/3 cup heavy cream
1 teaspoon dry mustard
1/2 teaspoon salt
1/8 teaspoon pepper

2 tablespoons bacon fat
1/3 cup chopped onion
3/4 cup broccoli chopped into small bite-sized pieces
12 ounces of country ham, rinsed and chopped
1 1/2 cup shredded cheddar cheese (more if you like)

Mix the first five ingredients until well blended. A Ninja or blender works well. Set aside. Cook the onion and broccoli in a cast iron skillet until tender. Add the chopped ham and remove from heat. Spread the ham, broccoli, and onion evenly in the skillet. Sprinkle the cheese over the ham mixture. Pour the egg mixture over the dish. Bake at 350 degrees for 30 to 40 minutes until browned and set. Let cool for at least 10 minutes before serving. If you don't have a cast iron skillet, you can use a glass baking dish. You can also use a muffin tin for better portioning.

NUTRITION FACTS 8 servings. Per serving: Calories: 299.2; Fat: 21.5 grams; Protein 22.2 grams; Carbohydrate 2.6 grams; Fiber 0.25 grams

Mexican Chorizo Frittata

My husband does not like eggs, but he really enjoys this frittata. The hearty chorizo, jalapeno, cream cheese, and shredded cheese make it a great brunch recipe, especially if you're feeding a crowd that includes the fellas.
Video: http://bit.ly/CookingKetoWithKristieFrittata

INGREDIENTS

8 eggs

1/3 cup heavy cream

1 teaspoon dry mustard

1/2 teaspoon salt

1/8 teaspoon pepper

1 lb. chorizo, browned

1/4 cup onion, finely chopped

1/3 cup bell pepper, chopped

2 fresh jalapenos

1 1/2 cups shredded cheese (cheddar, cheddar jack, etc.)

4 ounces of cream cheese, in small cubes

Mix the first five ingredients until well blended. A Ninja or blender works well. Set aside. Cook the onion, bell pepper, jalapenos (if fresh), and chorizo in skillet until browned and vegetables are tender. Layer the chorizo cooked with onion and pepper into a 9" by 13" glass baking dish. Top with shredded cheese. If using jarred jalapenos, layer the slices over top of the cheese. Distribute the small cubes of cream cheese evenly over the dish. Pour the egg mixture over the meat and cheese. Use a fork to make sure that the egg mixture is mixed through the dish.

Bake at 350 degrees for 30 to 40 minutes until browned and set. Let cool for at least 10 minutes before serving. Serve with chopped fresh cilantro, avocado, and sour cream.

NUTRITION FACTS 8 servings. Per serving: Calories: 427.6263; Fat: 34.975 grams; Protein 22.7 grams; Carbohydrate 2.8 grams; Fiber 0 grams

Philly Cheesesteak Frittata

Bunless Philly Cheesesteaks are a quick go-to dinner for my family, so it just made sense to turn it into a breakfast meal. A bonus is that these warm up well for a quick meal on busy mornings.
Video: http://bit.ly/CookingKetoWithKristieFrittata

INGREDIENTS

8 eggs
1/3 cup heavy cream
1 teaspoon dry mustard
1/2 teaspoon salt
1 lb. Philly cheesesteak meat
1 tablespoon bacon fat
1 1/2 teaspoon minced garlic

1 teaspoon onion powder
1 teaspoon salt
1/2 cup bell pepper, sliced
1/3 cup onion, sliced
1 tablespoon Worcestershire sauce
1 1/2 cups cheddar cheese, shredded
1 cup mozzarella cheese, shredded

Mix the first four ingredients until well blended. Set aside. Cook the cheesesteak meat in the bacon fat with the garlic, onion powder, and salt until the meat is browned. Add the Worcestershire sauce, onion, and bell pepper and cook until just tender. Let cool. Spread the meat and vegetable mixture evenly into a 9" by 13" glass baking dish. Sprinkle the cheese over the top of the meat mixture. Pour the egg mixture over all of the filling. Use a fork to make sure that the egg mixture is mixed through the dish. Bake at 350 degrees for 30 to 40 minutes until browned and set. Let cool for at least 10 minutes before serving.

NUTRITION FACTS 8 servings. Per serving: Calories: 412; Fat: 31.8 grams; Protein 25.2 grams; Carbohydrate 2.6 grams; Fiber 0 grams

Creamed Chipped Beef

Creamed chipped beef is the stuff of my childhood! My very best friend while growing up had a precious mama who would make this just for us. Hers was the high carb version, and she warned us both about the calories, I knew that sleepovers at her house meant creamed chip beef on toast for breakfast. No toast here, but this is delicious over a slice of toasted Soul Bread or one of my low carb biscuit recipes. Each of those recipes is included in the section on breads.

INGREDIENTS

4 tablespoons butter
3 ounces cream cheese
2 cups beef broth
1 teaspoon Worcestershire sauce
1/2 teaspoon garlic

1/2 teaspoon pepper
4.5 ounces dried beef, chopped
2 teaspoon cold coffee or 1/4 teaspoon instant coffee granules (optional)
1/2 cup heavy cream
1/4 teaspoon glucomannan or xanthan gum

In a heavy sauce pan on medium low heat melt butter and cream cheese. Add beef broth. Use a whisk to blend until smooth. Add garlic powder, Worcestershire sauce, and pepper. Stir in chopped dried beef. Simmer on low heat for about 10 minutes or until mixture thickens. Stir frequently. Reduce heat and stir in coffee and heavy cream. Sprinkle in glucomannan a little at a time so that it doesn't clump. The mixture will thicken as it cools.

NUTRITION FACTS 8 servings. Per serving: Calories: 166.9; Fat: 15.6 grams; Protein 6.7 grams; Carbohydrate 1.7 grams; Fiber 0 grams

Savory Sausage Gravy

Sausage gravy is the ultimate breakfast comfort food. Spoon this warm, creamy gravy over eggs or Belle's Biscuit on page 126. "Diet food" can be delicious!
Video: http://bit.ly/CookingKetoWithKristieSausageGravy

INGREDIENTS

1 lb. sausage, cooked and crumbled
8 ounces cream cheese
1 1/2 cup heavy cream
1 teaspoon garlic powder

1 teaspoon onion powder
1 teaspoon instant coffee
1/4 teaspoon salt

Brown the sausage in a large skillet until well done and crumbled. Add the cream cheese and melt on medium low heat, stirring frequently. Add the heavy cream and the seasonings. You may want to thin the gravy with bone broth or additional cream. Serve with warm low carb biscuits or over eggs for a lower carb option.

NUTRITION FACTS 8 servings.
Per serving: Calories: 416.6; Fat: 39.5 grams; Protein 11.5 grams; Carbohydrate 2.4 grams; Fiber 0 grams

Breakfast Bombs

At 0.36 carbs each, these little flavor powerhouses are a delicious option. They are good warm or cold and travel really well. They're kinda cute too on a buffet for brunch or party. Make up a batch on the weekend, and you will have four perfect keto meals prepped for when you're on the run.

INGREDIENTS

1 lb. breakfast sausage, browned and crumbled

8 ounces cream cheese, softened

1/2 teaspoon salt

1/2 teaspoon garlic

3 eggs, soft scrambled

2 scallions, finely chopped

1 cup cheddar cheese, shredded

1 cup bacon pieces, divided into 1/2 cups

In a large bowl, combine the crumbled sausage, salt, garlic, and cream cheese. Mix thoroughly. Add the softly scrambled eggs, scallions, cheese, and half of the bacon pieces. Mix well with a spatula or wooden spoon. When well mixed, form 1 inch balls with the mixture. Roll each ball into the remaining bacon pieces to coat. May garnish with sprinkles of finely chopped scallions. For extra zest, add a finely chopped jalapeno to the mixture before forming the balls. These refrigerate well and make an excellent brunch option. Makes 36 balls.

NUTRITION FACTS 4 servings. Per serving: Calories: 792; Fat: 64.8 grams; Protein 43.6 grams; Carbohydrate 3.25 grams; Fiber 0.2 grams

Fathead Breakfast Pizza

Who doesn't love pizza for breakfast? Even the most hardened egg haters tend to enjoy this recipe. To save time, make several crusts ahead of time, bake, and freeze or refrigerate them. Add the toppings, bake, and impress all of your family and friends. Fathead is so filling that it's easy to get several meals from this recipe.

INGREDIENTS

Crust
1 1/2 cups shredded mozzarella
2 tablespoons cream cheese
1/3 cup almond flour
1/3 cup oat fiber
1 egg
1 teaspoon garlic salt
1 teaspoon Italian seasoning

Pizza topping
4 ounces cream cheese, softened
1/2 teaspoon salt
1/4 teaspoon pepper
1/4 teaspoon onion powder
1/4 teaspoon garlic powder
4 ounces of Canadian bacon, chopped
1/2 lb. breakfast sausage, cooked
1/2 cup bacon pieces
1 cup fresh spinach (optional)
5 eggs, well beaten (or make sunny-side up)

Crust - Melt the cream cheese and mozzarella on medium heat on the stovetop or in the microwave. Mix well. Add the almond flour and oat fiber and incorporate into the melted cheese. It's easiest to do this by hand with well-oiled hands. If the "dough" becomes stringy, warm it again. Last, add the egg and seasonings and mix well. Note: You can lower the carb count to under 3 grams per serving by using crushed pork rinds in place of the almond flour and the oat fiber. You may also use 1/2 cup of almond flour and omit the oat fiber.

Line a jelly roll baking sheet with parchment paper. Use your hands to flatten the dough or put a second piece of parchment paper on top of the dough and flatten it. Be sure to press the dough up the sides to make an edge. Bake the flattened dough at 350 degrees for 10 to 12 minutes or until browned. When browned, remove from oven and let cool.

Topping - Mix the cream cheese and spices until smooth and well blended. Set aside. Spread the cream cheese mixture over the pizza crust. Distribute the Canadian bacon, sausage, bacon, and spinach evenly over cream cheese layer. Slowly and carefully pour the beaten eggs over the pizza, covering edge to edge. You can also crack the eggs over the pizza and bake them "sunny side" up instead of mixing. Bake at 350 degrees until set, about 15 minutes. Let cool for 10 minutes before slicing and serving.

Photo courtesy of Sondy Murray

NUTRITION FACTS 6 servings. Per serving: Calories: 450; Fat: 34.4 grams; Protein 28.8 grams; Carbohydrate 3.8 grams; Fiber 0.78 grams

Faux-gurt

Few people would think of yogurt as an unhealthy breakfast choice. On a ketogenic diet, however, commercial yogurt is often too high in sugar and carbs. Some "plain" brands can have 12 to 15 grams of carbohydrate in a one cup serving. Since low carb yogurt is hard to find, I have found a few excellent low carb alternatives to yogurt.

Below is a list of products that behave like yogurt and make an excellent substitute when combined and lightly sweetened with a few low carb berries like blackberries, raspberries, or blueberries. The table provides a guide. The only brand I have found that is low enough in carbs for me is White Mountain Bulgarian yogurt. Please check the serving size and macronutrients for the brands you use.

Alternative	Serving Size	Fat Grams	Protein Grams	Carbohydrate Grams
Crème fraiche	28 grams	11 grams	<1 grams	<1 grams
Sour cream	30 grams	6 grams	1 grams	1 grams
Marscapone	14 grams	6 grams	<1 grams	0 grams
White Mountain Bulgarian yogurt	1 cup	8 grams	13 grams	5 grams

To make faux-gurt, you want to maximize fat and flavor while keeping carbs very low. Any of the three options below make a great faux-gurt.

Option 1: Mix 1/2 cup of full fat White Mountain Bulgarian yogurt and 4 tablespoons of crème fraiche. This yields 26 grams of fat, 7 grams of protein, and fewer than 4 total carbs which in low enough in carbs to allow a for a few berries. This is a deliciously creamy high fat option that also includes the bite and probiotics of whole yogurt. Sour cream can be used instead of cream fraiche; however, the macros will change.

Option 2: Mix crème fraiche with mascarpone. Mascarpone brings a really nice texture to crème fraiche and makes a really delicious faux yogurt option that is thicker than using crème fraiche or sour cream alone. Using 3 servings of cream fraiche to 2 servings of mascarpone gives you 45 grams of fat, 4 grams of protein, and fewer

than 3 grams of carbohydrates. It's a delicious breakfast fat bomb when you add just a bit of your preferred sweetener and a few berries.

Option 3: Use full fat sour cream as yogurt. Once you add a little sweetener and berries, it makes a surprisingly tasty substitute for yogurt. Using 1/2 cup of sour cream gives you 24 grams of fat, 4 grams of protein, and 4 grams of carbohydrate.

{ almond flour }

Perfect Keto Pancakes

Don't let the long list of ingredients intimidate you. These have the BEST flavor and are well worth the effort. We tend to make these on the weekends and refrigerate the leftovers for a quick breakfast during the week. These warm perfectly in a toaster. The macros make them a perfect keto option because of the higher fat, moderate protein, and lower carb count.

Video: http://bit.ly/CookingKetoWithKristieAlmondFlourPancakes

INGREDIENTS

3/4 cup heavy cream
2 tablespoons apple cider vinegar
1 cup finely ground almond flour
1/3 cup crushed pork rinds
1/3 cup plus 2 tablespoons whey protein isolate, or egg white protein powder, vanilla or unflavored
2 tablespoons oat fiber (or 1 tablespoon coconut flour)

2 tablespoons melted butter
1/2 cup full fat sour cream
2 eggs
1 1/2 teaspoon baking powder
1/2 teaspoon baking soda
1/4 teaspoon salt
1 teaspoon vanilla
1/3 cup granulated sweetener (Sukrin :1)
10 drops liquid sweetener

First, add the vinegar to the heavy cream and set it aside to make "buttermilk". In a large bowl or blender mix all of the ingredients except the buttermilk. Add the heavy cream and vinegar "buttermilk" last. Let sit for 10 minutes before frying. May add 2 tablespoons of coconut flour instead of pork rinds.

Fry batter on medium high heat in three inch diameter pancakes in your favorite oil such as butter, ghee, or coconut oil. Serve warm. The batter can also be used in a toaster oven.

NUTRITION FACTS 8 servings. Per serving: Calories: 321; Fat: 27.8 grams; Protein 13.5 grams; Carbohydrate 4.3 grams; Fiber 1.5 grams

Photo courtesy of Kim Hardie

{*nut free*}

Pork Rind Protein Pancakes

You hate pork rinds? No, you don't. You just need to try them as pancakes! Trust me. These have the flavor of French toast and a carb count you won't believe at fewer than 2 carbs per serving. The fat grams per serving are slightly less than the protein grams per serving, so you might want to add plenty of melted butter over the top of your short stack. Oh the problems of a ketogenic eater!

INGREDIENTS

1 cup of pork rinds, pulverized into a fine dust
1/3 cup whey protein isolate (plain or vanilla)
1/2 teaspoon baking powder
2 eggs, beaten
1/2 cup heavy cream

1/2 cup granulated sweetener
(Sukrin :1)
1 teaspoon vanilla extract
1 teaspoon cinnamon

Use a blender or Ninja to pulverize the pork rinds. Use a whisk to mix the pork rinds, whey protein isolate, and baking powder. In a second bowl, mix eggs, cream, cinnamon, extract, and sweetener. Add the dry ingredients and mix well. The mixture will thicken as it sits.

Heat a skillet on medium heat. Add ghee or coconut oil until melted. Drop small scoops of the batter into the skillet to make small pancakes, no more than 3.5" in diameter, and fry on medium heat. When browned, use a wide spatula to flip them and brown on the other side. Serve warm.

NUTRITION FACTS 4 servings. Per serving: Calories: 295.3; Fat: 20 grams; Protein 24.3 grams; Carbohydrate 2 grams; Fiber 0.3 grams

Kristie's Favorite Blueberry Cream Cheese Muffins

Blueberries are one of the few fruits I eat on a ketogenic diet, and I use them sparingly to keep the carb count low. Even with the berries, the carb count is under 2 total carbs, which makes these a fantastic low carb option. You can also omit the blueberries and the blueberry extract and use any combination of flavors such as cinnamon and pecan or cranberries and walnuts for variety.

Video: http://bit.ly/CookingKetoWithKristieBlueberryMuffin

INGREDIENTS

Dry Ingredients
1/3 cup whey protein isolate
1/3 cup oat fiber (or 2 tablespoons coconut flour)
1/3 cup finely ground almond flour
1 1/2 teaspoon baking powder
1 tsp glucomannan or xanthan gum
1/4 teaspoon salt

Wet ingredients
4 ounces butter, salted
3/4 cup granulated sweetener (Sukrin :1)
4 ounces cream cheese
3 eggs, added one a time
1/3 cup sour cream
1 teaspoon vanilla extract
1 teaspoon blueberry extract
17 grams dried blueberries or 1/3 cup fresh or frozen berries, drained

Mix the dry ingredients with a whisk and set aside. Using a stand or hand mixer, whip the cold butter until creamy. Add granulated sweetener and blend until mixture is lighter in color. Add cream cheese and blend well. Add eggs one at a time, mixing well after each addition. Stir in sour cream and extracts by hand. Add the dry ingredients to the wet ingredients and blend lightly. Do not over mix. Drop into muffin tin lined with 12 paper liners. You can bake them two different ways. You can bake at 375 degrees for about 10 minutes and then reduce the temperature to 350 for an additional 8 to 10 minutes. Alternately, you can bake at 350 degrees for 18 to 20 minutes. The muffins are done when slightly brown and slightly firm to the touch. These freeze really well.

NUTRITION FACTS 12 servings. Per serving: Calories: 164; Fat: 14.3 grams; Protein 5.5 grams; Carbohydrate 1.9 grams; Fiber 0.4 grams

Everything Nice Pumpkin Spice Muffins

{nut free}

Admittedly, I'm not a pumpkin spice fan, but these moist and flavorful muffins have won my heart. They are easy to make and have a fantastic texture. At under four total carbs each, high fat, and moderate protein, they make mornings very good indeed. Don't forget to add the cinnamon and brown sugar substitute to the tops.

Video: http://bit.ly/CookingKetoWithKristiePumpkinSpiceMuffins

INGREDIENTS

4 ounces butter, room temp	1/4 teaspoon salt
4 ounces cream cheese	1 1/2 teaspoon vanilla extract
3/4 cup Sukrin Gold, brown sugar substitute	1/2 teaspoon maple extract (optional)
5 eggs	1 teaspoon pumpkin pie spice
1/2 cup pumpkin puree	1/2 teaspoon cinnamon
1/3 cup coconut flour	1/4 teaspoon ground cloves (optional)
1/4 cup oat fiber	1/4 cup heavy cream
1 1/2 teaspoons baking powder	5 drops of liquid sweetener, if desired
1/2 teaspoon glucomannan	Additional Sukrin Gold and cinnamon for tops (optional)

Blend the cream cheese and butter until it is creamy and well blended. Add Sukrin Gold and blend. Add eggs one at a time, beating well after each addition. Beat in pumpkin puree. Set aside. Mix dry ingredients, including coconut flour, oat fiber, baking powder, glucomannan, and salt. By hand, blend dry ingredients with wet ingredients. Add next 5 ingredients and mix well. Add cream and liquid sweetener to taste.

Portion batter into a 12-cup muffin tin, filling 3/4 full. Sprinkle tops with a mix of Sukrin Gold and cinnamon. Bake at 350 degrees for 20 to 24 minutes. Remove from heat and let cool. Taste and texture is best after 30 minutes out of the oven. My favorite way to eat these is with some marscapone or warmed with some softened butter. Enjoy!

NUTRITION FACTS 12 servings. Per serving: Calories: 160; Fat: 13.9 grams; Protein 4.1 grams; Carbohydrate 3.9 grams; Fiber 1.5 grams

"Just like the real thing" Chocolate Chip Muffins

The first time I made these, Grace was my taste tester. She exclaimed, "Mom, these are just like the real thing!" and the name stuck. It's important to have "normal" foods for my family, but I want those foods to be part of a healthy ketogenic lifestyle. These muffins bring the best of both worlds with great ratios of fat to protein to carbohydrates.

Video: http://bit.ly/CookingKetoWithKristieChocolateChipMuffins

INGREDIENTS

1/3 cup whey protein isolate	4 ounces of butter, room temp
1/3 cup oat fiber (or 2 tablespoons coconut flour)	3/4 cup Sukrin + granulated sweetener
1/3 cup almond flour	4 ounces full fat cream cheese
1 1/2 teaspoon baking powder	3 eggs
1 teaspoon glucomannan (optional)	1/3 cup sour cream
1/4 teaspoon salt	2 teaspoons of vanilla extract
	3/4 cup low carb chocolate chips

Mix dry ingredients with a whisk and set aside. Cream butter and sugar together. When butter is lighter in color, add cream cheese. Make sure all is well-blended and smooth. Add eggs, one at a time, mixing well after each. Add sour cream and vanilla extract. When wet ingredients are well blended, stir dry ingredients into the wet ingredients by hand. Taste for sweetness. Add chocolate chips. Bake in muffin tins at 350 degrees for 14 to 16 minutes. Makes 12 muffins. These freeze well and make a great "treat" to throw in lunch boxes.

NUTRITION FACTS 12 servings. Per serving: Calories: 183; Fat: 9.9 grams; Protein 6.1 grams; Carbohydrate 1.8 grams; Fiber 0.5 grams

No Apple Spice Bread

No apples were hurt in the making of these muffins! Don't let the long list of ingredients fool you. This is very easy to make and worth every effort. All of the seasonings and extracts work together for maximum flavor and minimal carbohydrates. Don't tell the family there are no apples. Let them think you're "cheating".

INGREDIENTS

For the "apples"

1 1/2 cup zuchinni, peeled and chopped
1 teaspoon cinnamon
1 teaspoon vanilla extract
1 teaspoon apple extract
1 teaspoon apple pie spice
5 drops liquid sweetener

For the bread

1 cup hazelnut flour (or almond flour)
1/3 cup oat fiber
1/3 cup coconut flour (or whey protein isolate)
1 1/2 teaspoon baking powder

1 teaspoon salt
2 teaspoons cinnamon
2 teaspoons apple pie spice
4 ounces cream cheese, softened
6 ounces butter, softened
1 cup Sukrin Gold brown sugar sub
(or 3/4 cup granulated sweetener)
5 eggs
1/3 cup sour cream
1 1/2 teaspoon apple extract
1 teaspoon vanilla extract
1/2 cup chopped pecans (or walnuts)

Make "apples" by mixing the zucchini with the spices, extracts, and seasonings. Set aside. You can also cook these in a sauce pan on low heat with four ounces of butter and a couple of teaspoons of water to make stewed "apples" and serve it as a separate side.

Mix dry ingredients with a whisk and set aside. Use a hand mixer to blend cream cheese and butter. Mix well and add sweetener. When well blended and creamy, add eggs one at a time mixing well after each. By hand, stir in sour cream, extracts, and liquid sweetener. Taste for sweetness. Add in "apples" and nuts. Pour into two greased load pans 4.5' by 8". You may also grease the loaf pans and line with parchment paper. Bake at 350 degrees for

35 to 40 minutes. Center should be set and a toothpick should come out clean when inserted in the center. These may also be baked in muffin tins.

NUTRITION FACTS 16 servings. Per serving: Calories: 166; Fat: 14.6 grams; Protein 4.4 grams; Carbohydrate 4.6 grams; Fiber 2 grams

Keto Friendly Hot Chocolate

My grandmother always made the best hot chocolate. She started with cocoa powder and water, and I loved when she made it for me. Sadly, my own children got cocoa mixes until we went low carb, and I was determined to make my own. This is essentially my grandmother's recipe with low carb sweetener instead of sugar. My kids, and their friends, think it is as special as I did, especially when I add a dollop or freshly whipped cream to the top.

INGREDIENTS

1 tablespoon cocoa powder

8 ounces hot water

1/4 cup heavy cream

1 tablespoon granulated sweetener or 3 drops liquid sweetener (Sukrin:1)

1/8 teaspoon vanilla extract (optional)

1/8 teaspoon instant coffee granules (optional)

In a small saucepan, heat 8 ounces of hot water until boiling. Remove from heat. Stir in cocoa powder until completely dissolved. Add in heavy cream, sweetener to taste, vanilla and instant coffee if desired. Return to low heat until hot. Add 1 full teaspoon of instant coffee for mocha flavor.

NUTRITION FACTS 1 serving. Per serving: Calories: 224; Fat: 21.5 grams; Protein 3.5 grams; Carbohydrate 3.2 grams; Fiber 2 grams

Low Carb Hazelnut Coffee Creamer

This recipe is for those who like a little coffee with their cream and a lot of flavor. Hazelnut oil is a monounsaturated fat and 74% omega 9. It's a relatively good fat that you're adding. Also, hazelnut oil is excellent used in "nutella" flavored cookies and cakes like my No-tella Muffin on page 149. I promise you'll use the hazelnut oil and hazelnut extracts in other recipes. This makes two generous servings. You may get four servings from one batch.

INGREDIENTS

3 ounces heavy cream

1 1/4 teaspoon hazelnut oil

1/2 teaspoon hazelnut extract

6 drops liquid sweetener

Mix all ingredients with a blender or immersion blender to incorporate the oil and cream. Be sure to blend it well when you make it and store it in the refrigerator. If it separates in the fridge, blend it again before adding to your coffee.

NUTRITION FACTS 2 servings. Per serving: Calories: 170.5; Fat: 17.8 grams; Protein 1.5 grams; Carbohydrate 0.9 grams; Fiber 0 grams

Creamy Pumpkin Spice Coffee

Every year the third season, Pumpkin Spice Everything season, brings a craving for warm pumpkin spice coffee. Be sure to use a blender to get all of the creamy goodness of buttered coffee. You can also enjoy this as a meal by adding an extra tablespoon of butter or coconut oil.

INGREDIENTS

12 ounces freshly brewed coffee
1 tablespoon butter
1 tablespoon pumpkin
1/4 teaspoon pumpkin pie spice
1/8 teaspoon ginger

1/4 teaspoon cinnamon
1/4 teaspoon vanilla extract
2 tablespoons heavy cream
Sweetener to taste

Add butter, pumpkin, spices, extract, and heavy cream to your favorite freshly brewed coffee. Add sweetener to taste. Mix in a blender or use an immersion blender to mix until frothy. Add a dollop of whipped cream and sprinkle cinnamon on top for a special treat.

NUTRITION FACTS 1 servings. Per serving: Calories: 202; Fat: 22.54 grams; Protein 1.17 grams; Carbohydrate 1.84 grams; Fiber 0.4 grams

When he became too weary to howl, his father
staggered out, blinking, into the light. I believe you
son, his father said, and he strode away toward the
weed heads and wildflowers with his planted crop

Odell walked into the house and packed a satchel
safe box in his father's office he took all the cash
pouch of gold pieces and a stack of paper bills. He
room and took a diamond and ruby brooch, an emerald
of pearls. He went and saddled his horse and rode

In the years before the war, he searched the cotton
to find Lucinda, and he had never set foot on home

In a sense, he was still searching. This was the reason
came necessary to make money, he chose a traveling
business had eventually fallen from tradesman
picture himself
ing little

Chapter 2
BEYOND BACON

The focus of this book is really the main dishes. These are the foods that will help you sustain this lifestyle long-term. When I began low carb high fat, I made a commitment to making two new recipes each week. Pinterest helped me organize the recipes and after I made a recipe, I moved it to a special board and made notes in the comments about whether my family liked it or not and how I might change the recipe in the future. By creating that arsenal of new recipes, I also created new habits that helped this become a lifestyle that we could continue. I hope that these recipes will do the same for your family and that you will find them not only delicious, but also easy enough to include in your weekly meal plans.

These recipes should help you create meals that will not only feed your family dinner, but also most of them are great warmed up for lunch or even breakfast. I've tried to include recipes with simple ingredients that are easy to find. Each of these recipes is a favorite of my family, and many of them are low carb versions of high carb favorites familiar to all of us like chicken pot pie, chili, and meatloaf. Some recipes put old favorites together in new ways such as Cheeseburger Bites and Rueben casserole. Many of these recipes are great for sharing at any type of get-togethers. Taco Bake, crab dip, chicken wings, pizza casserole, and carnitas are always the first dishes to be emptied at home and away. I've also included ethnic dishes for variety and because my family loves those recipes. Last, there are some several hearty salads for summertime or to prepare on the weekend for busy week day lunches. Those include egg salad, chicken salad, seafood salad, salmon salad and others. Each is different and using ingredients that are easy to find.

You might also notice that many of my recipes are what I call "One Pot Wonders", meaning they can be made with one large skillet or pot which also makes them easier to make and easier to clean up after. When possible, I've included instructions for using a crockpot or for prepping these dishes ahead of time so that it's easier to stay on plan when you're busy. Most of these recipes are made in proportions to serve a family and to have leftovers. You can easily cut these meals in half if you aren't cooking for a family.

Basic Bone Broth

Whether it's chicken broth or beef bone broth, homemade bone broth is a wonderful whole food to have on hand. My freezer is typically stocked with both. My broth is very basic: Bones, water, and ACV. I don't add vegetables as it does increase the carb count. I prefer to add the vegetables I want as I use the broth to drink or in soups and stews.
Video: http://bit.ly/CookingKetoWithKritsiteBoneBroth

INGREDIENTS

Beef Broth	**Chicken Broth**
2.5 lbs beef bones	2 lbs chicken bones, necks, feet
2 quarts water	2 quarts water
1 tablespoon apple cider vinegar	1 tablespoon apple cider vinegar
1 tablespoon salt	1 tablespoon salt

-For beef broth, I like to use a mix of beef bones that include bones with marrow and bones that include joints.
-For chicken broth, adding the feet is what gives it the most gelatin. If you can't find chicken feet, don't worry about it, but do try to include neck bones or wings if you can.

Once you have the bones, you can use a stockpot, instant pot, or slow cooker to make broth. Add the bones, water, ACV, and salt to the crockpot, instant pot, or stockpot. I prefer using a slow cooker and letting the bones cook on low heat for 36 to 48 hours.
If using a stockpot on the stovetop, simmer on low for 12 hours.
If using an instant pot, use the pressure setting for 30 minutes to an hour, depending on your appliance. The broth is "done" when the bones become soft. As I test, I typically crush the bones between my fingers. If they crumble, then I know I've gotten the goodness out of them.

Strain the broth with a wire strainer or coffee filter, and store in the fridge or freezer. Broth will keep up to two weeks in the fridge or six months in the freezer.

NUTRITION FACTS 1 cup. Per serving:
Calories: 40; Fat: 6 grams; Protein 3.6 grams;
Carbohydrate 0.5 grams; Fiber 0 grams

Chicken No-noodle Soup

Chicken Noodle Soup is one of those classic comfort foods that is documented to help fight colds and flu. I'm convinced the "magic" is in the broth and not in the doughy noodles. We use Miracle noodles made from glucomannan or konjac, which does not impact blood glucose. If you can't find those or don't care for them, you can use zuchinni noodles or cabbage.

INGREDIENTS

2 quarts homemade chicken broth

3 tablespoons butter

2 stalks celery, chopped

1 tablespoon garlic, minced

2 tablespoons dried minced onion

4 cups cooked chicken, shredded

2 teaspoons dried parsley

2 packages Miracle noodles fettucine, drained, rinsed and cut into bite-sized pieces

1 medium carrot, finely chopped

1 teaspoon salt

1/4 teaspoon pepper

Melt butter in a large pot. Add celery, onion, and garlic and cook for three to four minutes. Add broth, carrot, parsley, salt, and pepper. Simmer until vegetables are tender. Add cooked chicken and Miracle noodles. Simmer for an additional 10 to 12 minutes before serving.

You can use zucchini noodles instead of Miracle noodles, but be sure to adjust the carb count. Also, add them only in the last 4 to 5 minutes before serving so that they hold together. If cooked too long, they will disintegrate. One cup of shredded cabbage also works well as "noodles" and is lower in carbs than zuchinni.

NUTRITION FACTS 8 servings. Per serving: Calories: 213.8; Fat: 15.2 grams; Protein 15 grams; Carbohydrate 2.7 grams; Fiber 0.7 grams

Photo courtesy of Lori Bartell Weed

Sausage & Kale Zuppa Toscana

My daughter asks for this hearty soup even when it's summer and not "soup weather". I use zucchini in place of potatoes to keep the carb count as low as possible since kale is higher carb than you might expect.
Video: http://bit.ly/CookingKetoWithKristieSausageandKaleSoup

INGREDIENTS

- 2 lbs. of Italian sausage
- 1/2 cup chopped onion
- 1 clove garlic
- 4 cups broth or bouillon
- 2 cups chopped zucchini
- 3 cups of chopped kale
- 1 cup heavy cream
- 1/3 cup grated parmesan cheese
- bacon pieces (optional)

Brown Italian sausage in a heavy stockpot. Add chopped onion, one clove garlic, salt, and pepper. After onion has browned, add broth (homemade bone broth or bouillon and water). Add chopped zucchini. Simmer for 15-20 minutes or until the zucchini is tender, and add chopped kale. Simmer for an additional 10 minutes and add one cup of heavy whipping cream. Keep on low heat so that the cream does not separate. Add grated parmesan and/or chopped bacon just before serving.

NUTRITION FACTS 8 servings. Per serving: Calories: 347.2; Fat: 30.3 grams; Protein 15.6 grams; Carbohydrate 4.7 grams; Fiber 0.6 grams

Hearty Three-Meat Chili

A hearty chili warms the spirit. Using three different meats helps add texture so that you won't miss the high carb beans included in traditional chili. A word of caution, exactly half of the carbs in this recipe come from the spices. Chili powder, garlic, cumin each have carbohydrates. I've measured them carefully to get the maximum flavor and the minimum impact on blood glucose. Be sure to add the butter as it not only helps to balance the ratio of proteins and fats, but butter always makes it better!
Video: http://bit.ly/CookingKetoWithKristie3MeatChili

INGREDIENTS

1 lb ground beef
1 lb cubed pork (or sausage)
1 lb round steak (cut into bite-sized pieces)
1 1/2 cups strained tomatoes (lowest carb count possible)
2 cups beef bone broth
4 ounces butter
1 cup water

2 tablespoons dried minced onion (or 1/2 cup fresh chopped)
2 teaspoons garlic
2 teaspoons salt
3 tablespoons chili powder
2 teaspoons cumin
2 teaspoons paprika
1 teaspoons onion powder

Brown the meats in a large pot. Add the onion and spices and cook until the onions begin to brown. Add a little broth or some of the butter if you need moisture as you brown the onions. Add the tomatoes, remaining bone broth, butter, and water. Simmer for 30 to 45 minutes. Enjoy with cheese and sour cream.

NUTRITION FACTS 8 servings. Per serving: Calories: 322.4; Fat: 22.5 grams; Protein 24.3 grams; Carbohydrate 5.1 grams; Fiber 1.5 grams

Kristie's Low Carb Brunswick Stew {BBQ Vegetable Soup}

In the barbecue belt, Brunswick stew is a staple. There are regional variations that include rabbit and other meats, but I make mine with leftover smoked meats. Think of it as a BBQ Vegetable Soup. This recipe, like many of my others, was inspired by a request from Grace and David. The traditional version includes sweetened BBQ sauces and added sugars. This version is a much healthier option.

Video: http://bit.ly/CookingKetoWithKristieBrunswickStew

INGREDIENTS

1.5 lbs chopped smoked meat (pulled pork BBQ, brisket, chicken, or any combination)

2 cups beef bone broth

2 tablespoons minced onion (or 1/3 cup fresh chopped)

1 can green beans, drained

1/2 cup cabbage, chopped into strips

1 cup chopped zucchini

1/4 cup chopped jicama or water chestnuts (for crunch but optional)

4 ounces butter

1/2 teaspoon garlic

1/2 cup Low Carb BBQ sauce (make my homemade sauce on page 109)

1/2 cup vinegar based BBQ sauce

1/2 cup strained tomatoes

Add all ingredients to a large pot or crockpot and simmer on medium to low heat until the vegetables are tender and the stew thickens, about 45 minutes to an hour. If you're using a crockpot, cook on low heat for 4 to 6 hours.

NUTRITION FACTS
8 servings. Per serving: Calories: 302.6; Fat: 21.4 grams; Protein 24.2 grams; Carbohydrate 4.3 grams; Fiber 1.3 grams

Gumbalaya

We fondly call this Gumbalaya because it's a little bit gumbo and a little bit jambalaya, but a lot delicious. Very hearty with a thick broth, chicken, kielbasa, and shrimp, it has just a few veggies--onion, bell pepper, and okra. We prefer it in a big bowl like a thick stew. It can be served over riced cauliflower, but be careful with the added carbohydrates since this recipe is 6.7 carbs for 1/8th of the entire recipe.
Video: http://bit.ly/CookingKetoWithKristieGumbalaya

INGREDIENTS

2 tablespoons bacon fat (coconut oil, mct oil, olive oil)
1 1/2 lbs cubed chicken breast
1 teaspoons minced garlic
1 small onion, chopped
1/2 cup green pepper, chopped
3 stalks celery, chopped
1 cup frozen chopped okra
28 ounce can crushed tomatoes

1/2 cup water
2 cups bone broth
1 teaspoon salt
1 teaspoon Cajun seasoning
1/8 teaspoon cayenne
12 ounce Pederson kielbasa, thinly sliced
2 lbs shrimp
1 teaspoon Zatarain's Pure Ground Gumbo File

Melt the bacon fat in a large cast iron skillet or other large skillet. Add the cubed chicken at garlic. Saute the chicken until browned. Add the onion and green pepper and cook with the chicken until the vegetables are tender. Add salt, Cajun seasoning, and cayenne. Stir the seasonings into the chicken and continue to cook. Add the kielbasa and stir in. Next, add celery and cook until tender. Stir in the okra and tomatoes. Add bone broth and stir. Return to simmering before adding shrimp. After the shrimp turn pink, add the ground gumbo file, stir well, and serve immediately. You don't want the shrimp to overcook.

NUTRITION FACTS 8 servings. Per serving: Calories: 543.3; Fat: 28.6 grams; Protein 59.4 grams; Carbohydrate 6.7 grams; Fiber 2.4 grams

Steamy Seafood Chowder

The high fat profile of this soup makes it an excellent keto meal. Because the seafood doesn't need to cook very long, it is also quick and easy enough to make for a weeknight meal. This is one of my personal favorites because I love seafood. You can also adapt this recipe to use chicken if you aren't a fan of seafood.
Video: http://bit.ly/CookingKetoWithKristieSeafoodChowder

INGREDIENTS
4 tablespoons butter
1/2 medium sized onion, chopped
2 cups chopped cauli (include stalks)
2 cups broth (chicken or seafood stock)
1/2 cup white wine
1/4 cup chopped bacon
1/4 tsp salt

1 cup heavy cream
1 teaspoon garlic powder
1 tablespoon dried parsley
3 ounces cream cheese
1 package Trader Joe's seafood blend (or mix of shrimp, scallops, clams)
8 ounces crab claw meat
1/4 cup sun-dried tomatoes finely chopped (optional)

Add butter and onion to a large stock pot and brown the onion. When browned, add garlic, parsley, and cauli. Brown thoroughly and then add the white wine, bone both, and cream cheese. Stirring frequently, simmer for 5-7 minutes on medium to low heat until the cream cheese is melted and all is well mixed. The cauliflower should be tender, but not mushy.

Add 1 cup of heavy cream and return to a low simmer. Add the seafood. Let simmer for 6-8 minutes until seafood is cooked. Served with freshly grated parmesan and bacon pieces.

NUTRITION FACTS 8 servings. Per serving: Calories: 336.9; Fat: 27.2 grams; Protein 16.3 grams; Carbohydrate 6.6 grams; Fiber 1.4 grams

Kristie's Crack Slaw

Not only does Grace request Crack Slaw about once per week, but her friends now request it too. I frequently make a batch on the weekends, so that she can have it for school lunches. I love that her friends are often envious of her "diet" lunches. I also love that this dish is inexpensive, quick, and cooked in one large skillet. Lots of reasons why you will find this addictive too.

Video: http://bit.ly/CookingKetowithKristieCrackSlaw

INGREDIENTS

2 lbs ground beef

1 tablespoon bacon fat

1 tablespoon dried onion

1/2 teaspoon salt

1 tablespoon toasted sesame oil

2 tablespoons ginger

1 teaspoon garlic powder

1/4 cup coconut aminos (or soy sauce. Do not add salt if using soy sauce)

4 cups of cabbage cut into strips

Red pepper (optional)

3 drops liquid sweetener (optional)

In a large skillet, brown the ground beef with bacon fat. Add the dried onion, salt, toasted sesame oil, ginger, garlic powder, and coconut aminos. When the beef is browned, let it simmer to remove some of the moisture. Add the shredded cabbage and cook on medium high heat until tender. Taste and adjust seasonings as desired.

NUTRITION FACTS 6 servings. Per serving: Calories: 473.3; Fat: 31 grams; Protein 38 grams; Carbohydrate 6.3 grams; Fiber 1.3 grams

Cheeseburger Bombs

Take all the goodness of a bacon cheeseburger and made flavorful bombs perfect for dinner, lunch on the go, or a party table. These are great warmed or served cold. Use the low carb ketchup recipe on page 108 as a dipping sauce.

INGREDIENTS

1 lb ground beef 93% lean, cooked and crumbled

4 ounces cream cheese, softened

1/3 cup mayonnaise

1 teaspoon prepared mustard

2 tablespoon diced dill pickles

1 tablespoon dried minced onions

2 teaspoons Worcestershire sauce

2/3 cup bacon pieces, separated into 1/3 cup each

4 ounces shredded cheddar cheese

Brown the ground beef and crumble. Set aside. In a large bowl, mix the cream cheese, mayonnaise, mustard, dill pickles, minced onions, Worcestershire sauce, and 1/3 cup bacon pieces. Blend thoroughly. Add ground beef and mix well. Add shredded cheese. When mixture is well blended, shape into 1 1/2 inch balls. Roll balls into remaining bacon pieces to coat. Arrange cheeseburger bombs on a tray. Sprinkle with cheese and finely sliced chives or scallions to garnish. Makes 36 balls.

NUTRITION FACTS 1 ball.
Per serving: Calories: 92; Fat: 7.4 grams; Protein 7.5 grams; Carbohydrate 0.71 grams; Fiber 0.10 grams

Pizza Meatzza

When you're craving pizza, you realize that the best part are the toppings. Start with hamburger and ground sausage to make a meat crust and then top it with your traditional pizza favorites. That's a Meatzza, which is a very keto-friendly meal.

Video: http://bit.ly/CookingKetoWithKristieMeatzza

INGREDIENTS

Crust:

3/4 lb. 93% lean hamburger
1/2 lb. sausage
2 tablespoons dried minced onion
1 teaspoon Italian herb seasoning
1/2 teaspoon oregano
1/2 teaspoon basil
Pepper to taste
Salt to taste

Toppings:

4 ounces tomato sauce
1/3 cup Ricotta cheese (or shredded cheese of choice)
1 teaspoon Italian herb seasoning
1/4 teaspoon garlic powder
1 1/2 cup shredded mozzarella cheese
1/2 cup shredded parmesan cheese
3 ounces Pepperoni slices
1/4 cup onion, chopped
1/3 cup bell pepper, chopped
1/2 pound sausage
1/4 cup bacon bits

Combine the crust ingredients, making sure the seasonings are mixed well throughout. In a medium cast iron skillet or a 9" by 13" oven safe baking dish, spread the meat mixture evenly over the bottom and sides of the dish. The meat layer will be about 1/3 inch thick. Bake at 375 degrees for 30-35 minutes until done.

While the meat crust is in the oven, brown the remaining sausage with the onion and bell pepper until sausage is done and the veggies are tender. Set aside.

The meat crust may shrink during baking and may now just fill the bottom of the dish. Using a leaner ground beef or sausage will minimize shrinkage. Spread the tomato sauce over the cooked meat crust. Then place a layer of ricotta cheese on top. Sprinkle the remaining Italian herb seasoning and garlic on top. Add a layer pepperoni, sausage, and bacon bits on top of the ricotta cheese. Cover those layers with the remaining cheese and Italian herbs. Bake at 375 to 400 degrees for 25 – 30 minutes until the cheeses are melted and bubbling.

Let cool 10 minutes before serving.

NUTRITION FACTS

8 servings. Per serving:
Calories: 412.4; Fat: 33.2 grams; Protein 33.5 grams; Carbohydrate 3.2 grams; Fiber 0.5 grams

Italian Meatloaf

Meatloaf without the mystery meat is still meatloaf, right? Serve it with mashed cauliflower and you will never miss the carbs that I intentionally left out. This is one of those simple recipes that will likely get added to your monthly meal rotation. As it bakes the whole house smells like "Welcome home!", and that's my favorite smell.

INGREDIENTS

1 lb ground beef 93% lean
1 lb ground pork 96% lean
2 teaspoons Italian seasoning
1 teaspoon salt
1 teaspoon dried basil
1/2 teaspoon dried oregano
2 tablespoons dried minced onion

1 egg, beaten
1 teaspoon garlic powder
2 tablespoons heavy cream (optional)
1/2 cup tomato sauce
1 cup full fat mozzarella cheese, shredded

Mix all ingredients except tomato sauce and mozzarella cheese. Shape into two loaves and place in two 8.5 by 4.5 inch loaf pans. Spoon 1/4 cup of tomato sauce over each loaf. Top each with 1/2 cup of mozzarella cheese. Bake at 375 degrees for 30 to 35 minutes until meat is cooked throughout. Let cool for 10 to 15 minutes before slicing.

NUTRITION FACTS 8 servings. Per serving: Calories: 231.6; Fat: 11.6 grams; Protein 27.8 grams; Carbohydrate 2.5 grams; Fiber 0.3 grams

Photo courtesy of Kirk Pillen Photography

Greek Meat Balls
with Tzatziki Sauce

The fresh mint in these meatballs provides a slightly sweet flavor while the feta adds a salty taste. Together with lamb, these are a tasty treat for your tastebuds. We prefer them with tzatziki, a creamy cucumber-based sauce that is really good with the lamb and mint. The tzatziki recipe is on page 119.
Video: http://bit.ly/CookingKetoWithKristieGreekMeatballs

INGREDIENTS

1 3/4 lb ground beef (can use beef, lamb, or mixture beef & lamb)

1 pkg fresh or 9 oz frozen spinach, cooked and drained

1 tablespoon fresh mint chopped

2 teaspoons minced garlic

1/4 teaspoon salt

1 tablespoon dehydrated minced onion

4 ounces crumbled feta cheese

Mix all ingredients well. Shape into 1 inch round meatballs and place on a foil-lined baking sheet. Bake at 375 degrees for 12-15 minutes until done. These meatballs freeze well and can be frozen before or after baking. These are great to pull from the freezer and toss into a lunch box. Serve with tzatziki.

NUTRITION FACTS 6 servings. Per serving: Calories: 258; Fat: 18 grams; Protein 20.5 grams; Carbohydrate 3.2 grams; Fiber 1 grams

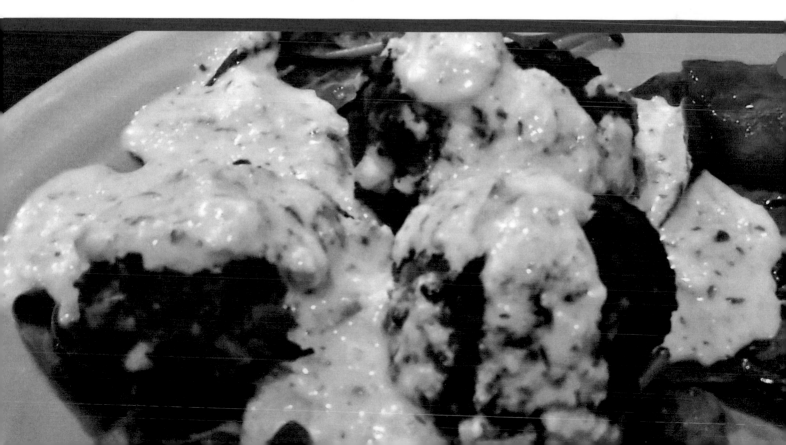

Skillet Taco Bake

Another great recipe for any large gathering or for a simple dinner eaten as a main dish. This recipe uses hamburger and Mexican sausage (chorizo) for an out of this world skillet bake. Serve it with fresh avocado, salsa or pico, and sour cream. You can also provide tortilla chips for the carbivores. Your guests will never know how simple it is--they will just think you're a culinary genius!
Video: http://bit.ly/CookingKetoWithKristieTacoBake

INGREDIENTS

1.25 lbs ground beef
1 lb Mexican sausage (chorizo)
1/2 cup of chopped onion
1/2 cup chopped green bell pepper
1/2 teaspoon salt
1 teaspoon garlic powder
1 teaspoon cumin

2 teaspoon chili powder
14-ounce can of crushed tomatoes (no sugar added)
3.5 ounce can green chilies
3 ounces cream cheese
3 cups shredded cheddar cheese

Brown ground beef and chorizo in a large oven proof skillet such as a cast iron skillet. Add onion and bell pepper and cook until the vegetables are tender. Add seasonings, crushed tomatoes, chilies, and cream cheese. Stir on medium low heat until the cream cheese melts and is thoroughly mixed. Sprinkle shredded cheddar cheese on top. Bake at 375 degrees for about 20 minutes or until hot and bubbly. Serve hot. Any leftovers are delicious warmed up and served with eggs sunny-side up.

NUTRITION FACTS 12 servings. Per serving: Calories: 337.8; Fat: 23.8 grams; Protein 24.3 grams; Carbohydrate 3.4 grams; Fiber 0.8 grams

Tomato Gravy with Pork

Italian comfort food begins with a rich tomato sauce with fatty chunks of pork ladled over creamy ricotta and baked until bubbly. The fatty pieces of pork I use come from stewed pork neck bones, which are tender and mild. You can use a different cut of pork or beef if you prefer.
Video: http://bit.ly/CookingKetoWithKristieTomatoGravy

INGREDIENTS

4 lbs. pork neck bones, stewed or roasted
17.64 ounce Pomi tomato sauce
14 ounce Fedeli whole tomatoes, pureed
2 teaspoons basil
3 cloves garlic
2 teaspoons oregano leaves
2 tablespoons Italian seasoning
2 tablespoons dehydrated minced onion
2 teaspoons salt
8 ounces ricotta cheese
2 cups shredded, mozzarella with 1/2 cup reserved for topping
1/2 cup grated fresh Parmesan

Roast the pork neck bones in a slow cooker with 1/4 cup of water. When the meat is cooked and tender, pick the meat from the bones and reserve the broth. Set aside. In a large pot, stir the tomato sauce and stained tomatoes on medium high heat. Add the pork meat and simmer. Strain 2 cups of the pork neck broth and add it to the tomato sauce and meat mixture. Add spices. Simmer uncovered on low heat for about 30 to 45 minutes or until thickened. In an oven safe skillet or 9" by 13" glass baking dish, spread a layer of ricotta cheese. Top the ricotta with a layer of shredded mozzarella. Pour the thickened tomato gravy and pork mixture over the ricotta and mozzarella layers. Add some shredded parmesan and mozzarella on top and sprinkle with a little dried basil or Italian seasonings. Bake at 375 degrees until the dish is bubbly and the cheeses melted. Let sit for at least 5 minutes before serving. Serve with low carb Italian flavored flatbread if desired.

NUTRITION FACTS
8 servings. Per serving: Calories: 225.8; Fat: 15.1 grams; Protein 14.1 grams; Carbohydrate 6.9 grams; Fiber 1.4 grams

Pizza Casserole

*Perfect for potlucks or brunch or football season, pizza casserole has the best of traditional pizza toppings.
Baked in a glass baking dish, it cuts easily into squares for serving or use a muffin tin for crispier edges and
smaller bite-sized servings.*

INGREDIENTS

6 ounces cream cheese, softened

2 eggs, beaten

1/3 cup parmesan cheese

1 1/2 teaspoon Italian seasoning

1/2 teaspoon garlic powder

3/4 teaspoon baking powder

16 ounces mozzarella cheese (reserve 4 ounces
for topping)

4 ounces pepperoni, chopped

8 ounces sausage, cooked and crumbled

2 tablespoons dried minced onion (optional)

2 tablespoons green bell pepper (optional)

Use a hand mixer to blend the cream cheese and eggs. Stir in the seasonings and cheeses. Mix well. Add the
pepperoni and cooked sausage. Top with the onion and bell pepper if using. Grease a 9" by 13" baking dish or a
large oven safe skillet and pour in the mixture. Top with reserved mozzarella cheese. Bake at 375 degrees for about
20 to 25 minutes until puffy and browned. Let stand at least 7 to 10 minutes before serving. A few tablespoons of
low carb marinara sauce drizzled over top is very good. You can also add black olives or any other favorite pizza
toppings.

NUTRITION FACTS 8 servings. Per serving: Calories: 300.4; Fat: 24.1 grams; Protein 14.8 grams;
Carbohydrate 2.1 grams; Fiber 0.1 grams

Philly Cheesesteak Casserole

When I first made this dish, my husband and daughter looked at it, looked at each other, and looked at me. Grace asked, "What's Plan B? Can we go get a burger?" I insisted they try it. Not only has it become a hit, but they argued over who would take the leftovers for lunch that week.

INGREDIENTS

2 lbs. beef, sliced or shredded

1 tablespoon ghee or bacon fat

1 cup bell pepper, sliced

1 cup onion, sliced

8 ounces mushrooms, sliced

2 cloves garlic, divided

2 teaspoons Italian seasoning, divided

1/2 teaspoon salt

1/2 teaspoon pepper

8 ounces cream cheese, softened

1/2 cup mayonnaise

2 tablespoons Worcestershire

2 cups cheddar cheese, shredded

12 ounces provolone cheese slices

In a large skillet on medium high heat, brown beef in ghee or bacon fat. When the meat is browned, add onions, pepper, mushrooms, garlic, salt, pepper, and 1 teaspoon of Italian seasonings. Continue cooking until vegetables are just tender, but not soft. Remove from heat and set aside. In a large bowl, mix cream cheese, mayonnaise, 1 teaspoon garlic, 1 teaspoon Italian seasoning, 2 tablespoons Worcestershire, and cheddar cheese. Add meat mixture and combine. Spoon into a 9" by 13" glass baking dish and top with the slices of provolone cheese. Bake at 375 degrees for 20 to 25 minutes or until bubbly and slightly browned.

NUTRITION FACTS 10 servings. Per serving: Calories: 427.2; Fat: 34.2 grams; Protein 28 grams; Carbohydrate 3.3 grams; Fiber 0.6 grams

Rueben Casserole

Using deli corned beef makes this a quick family favorite. The caraway seeds add an authentic Rueben sandwich taste that will make you think you're eating the classic hot sandwich.

Video: http://bit.ly/CookingKetoWithKristieRuebenCasserole

INGREDIENTS

1/2 cup mayonnaise	8 ounces sauerkraut
4 ounces cream cheese, softened	2 cups swiss cheese
1/2 cup homemade sugar free ketchup	1 teaspoon caraway seeds
2 tablespoons dill pickle, diced	16 ounces cooked corn beef, chopped
1/3 cup onion, finely grated	

In a large bowl, mix the cream cheese and mayonnaise until well combined. Add the ketchup, dill pickles, and onion. Mix thoroughly. When well mixed, add the remaining ingredients and stir until uniformly mixed. Spoon mixture into a greased glass baking dish, 9" inch diameter or 9" by 13". Bake at 350 degrees for 18 to 20 minutes until browned and bubbly.

NUTRITION FACTS 6 servings.
Per serving: Calories: 457; Fat: 39 grams;
Protein 24.9 grams; Carbohydrate 4.7 grams;
Fiber 0.8 grams

One Pot Chicken Pot Pie

My family refuses to eat leftover chicken unless I reinvent it. One Pot Chicken Pot Pie is a genius disguise for leftover chicken, transforming neglected leftovers into a comforting classic made in an old-fashioned skillet.
Video: http://bit.ly/CookingKetoWithKrisiteChickenPotPie

INGREDIENTS

1/3 cup chopped onion
1/3 cup chopped carrots (omit if too carby for you)
1/2 cup chopped broccoli stems (avoid the "florets)
3/4 cup chopped cauliflower
1 cup chopped zucchini
1 can green beans, drained
2 stalks chopped celery
1/3 cup sliced and chopped mushrooms

3 tablespoons butter
2 cups chicken bone broth
4 ounces cream cheese
1/2 cup heavy cream
1/2 teaspoon thyme
1/4 teaspoon salt
1/4 teaspoon pepper
1/4 teaspoon Bell's poultry seasoning
3 cups of cooked chicken
1/2 teaspoon glucomannan or xanthan gum (optional thickener)

One batch of Bell's Biscuits, recipe on page 126
or one batch of Miracle Biscuits, recipe on page 128

Sauté the vegetables (first 8 ingredients) in butter in a large cast iron skillet (or oven safe casserole) until the vegetables are tender. Add the chicken bone broth. Simmer until the bone broth is reduced (about 10 minutes). Add cream cheese and heavy cream and simmer on low heat until thickened. Using a lower heat will keep the cream from breaking. Add the remaining seasonings and mix well. Sprinkle the glucomannan or xanthan gum over this dish, being careful to add in gradually and to keep stirring so that it doesn't clump. Add the chicken and mix into the vegetables and sauce.

While the chicken pot pie filling is simmering, prepare the biscuit recipe. Once the filling is ready, drop the biscuit dough on top, covering the filling. (The miracle biscuit dough can be rolled out for a more traditional pie crust topping.) Bake at 350 to 375 degrees for about 20-22 minutes until biscuits are browned and not doughy underneath.

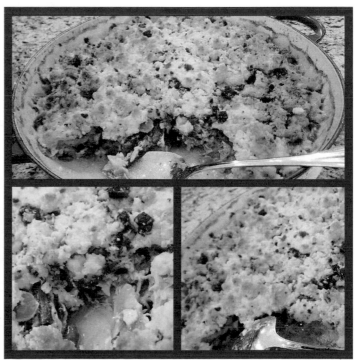

You can also add one cup of cheddar cheese, 1 teaspoon of garlic, and 1/3 cup chopped bacon to the biscuit dough. Using Belle's Biscuits adds an additional 3 carbs per serving, while using the Miracle Biscuit recipe adds an additional 1 carb per serving to the nutritional information.

NUTRITION FACTS 12 servings. Per serving:
Calories: 159.8; Fat: 10.7 grams; Protein 12.9 grams;
Carbohydrate 3.4 grams; Fiber 0.9 grams

Summer's Best Seafood Salad

This salad tastes like summer at the beach. It is the best of the sea combined with the cool crunch of cucumber, the creamy avocado, and the punch of fresh tomatoes. This is the summer salad you didn't know you should make!

INGREDIENTS

1 lb. cooked salmon, bite-sized pieces

1 lb. cooked shrimp, chopped

1/2 cup avocado, chopped

2 tablespoons lime juice

1/2 cup mayonnaise

1/3 cup sour cream

1 clove garlic

1 teaspoon salt

1/4 teaspoon white pepper

1/4 cup onion, finely minced

1/3 cup cucumber, chopped

1/3 cup tomato, chopped (optional)

In a mixing bowl, combine lime juice, mayonnaise, sour cream, garlic, salt, pepper, and minced onion. Set aside. In a larger bowl, toss together salmon, shrimp, avocado, cucumber, and tomato. Pour mayonnaise dressing over the seafood and vegetables and toss gently to combine. Let chill 20 to 30 minutes before serving.

NUTRITION FACTS 4 servings. Per serving: Calories: 473.6; Fat: 27.4 grams; Protein 49.3 grams; Carbohydrate 5 grams; Fiber 1.8 grams

Curried Chicken

Don't make this dish for company unless you don't mind them seeing you lick the sauce from your plate. Even my husband who has a strong aversion to coconut really enjoys this recipe. In fact, I named it Chicken Curry to hide the fact that it has coconut milk. He never detected the coconut flavor, but I did slip up and call it Coconut Chicken Curry at the dinner table. Fortunately, he had proclaimed it delicious before the truth was told.

INGREDIENTS

2 lbs boneless chicken breast cut into 3-inch pieces
2 tablespoons ghee or coconut oil
2 tablespoons curry powder
2 cloves garlic, minced
2 teaspoons ginger, grated

13.5 ounces Trader Joe's coconut milk
4 ounces tomato sauce
4 ounces chicken broth
1 tablespoon fish sauce (optional)
3 tablespoons butter, salted

In a large skillet, melt ghee or coconut oil on medium high heat. Add curry powder, garlic, and ginger and heat until fragrant. Add chicken, browning well on each side. When chicken is browned, add broth and scrape sides and bottom of pan to dissolve any browned seasonings into the broth. Add coconut milk, tomato sauce, and fish sauce. Simmer on low heat for 20 to 30 minutes. The chicken should be tender as it simmers, and the sauce will reduce. Add more chicken broth if the sauce becomes too thick. Add butter at the end of the cooking time just before serving.

NUTRITION FACTS 6 servings. Per serving: Calories: 202.8; Fat: 23.8 grams; Protein 16.4 grams; Carbohydrate 4.4 grams; Fiber 1.4 grams

Asian Chicken Skillet

Chinese food in American restaurants is typically full of sugars and starches, which makes it very difficult to eat Chinese unless you make it at home. This is a very basic recipe that will satisfy your cravings for Chinese take-out. Feel free to substitute beef for the chicken or use your favorite low carb vegetables.

Videos: http://bit.ly/CookingKetoWithKristieAsianChickenSkillet
http://bit.ly/CookingKetoWithKrisiteAsianBrownSauce

INGREDIENTS

Basic Asian Brown Sauce (for cooking chicken)
2 tablespoons sesame oil (or your favorite oil)
1 tablespoon fresh garlic
2 tablespoons fresh ginger
1/2 tablespoon fresh turmeric (optional)
3 lbs. chicken, cubed

Basic Brown Sauce (for cooking vegetables)
2 tablespoons rice vinegar (no sugar)
2 tablespoons sesame oil (optional)
1/2 cup coconut aminos (or tamari or soy sauce)
1 tablespoon ginger

Vegetables
1 cup fresh asparagus
1 cup fresh broccoli
1 1/2 cup fresh mushrooms
1 cup bean sprouts
1/2 teaspoon glucomannan or xanthan gum (thickening agent)

Heat oil in a large skillet or wok. Add garlic, ginger, and turmeric. Heat for a minute or so to get flavors from the spices. Keep the skillet on high heat. Cook chicken for about 20 minutes until brown. Add sauce to the chicken slowly and on the side of the skillet so as not to reduce the pan temperature too much. Let chicken simmer in the sauce for 10 to 15 minutes until it's tender and the sauce reduces. You can also cover the pan and let it simmer to be sure chicken is tender.

When the chicken is browned, add the vegetables, or cook the vegetables in a separate skillet (directions below). Cook the vegetables until crisp tender. When all is done, add 1/2 tsp of glucomannan and stir. Serve over Miracle Rice or cauli-rice and enjoy!

Use your favorite veggies, but mindful of the carb count in each. For this recipe I used asparagus, broccoli, bean sprouts, and mushrooms. Other good options include zuchinni, peppers, snow peas (small amounts), or onion (small amounts).

If you're using a separate skillet as I often do, make another recipe of brown sauce and add it to the vegetables. Keep on high heat and let the sauce reduce. The vegetables are done when they are crisp-tender. You don't want to the veggies to be too soft. Add to the chicken and enjoy!

NUTRITION FACTS 8 servings. Per serving:
Calories: 177; Fat: 8.9 grams; Protein 17.6 grams;
Carbohydrate 5.9 grams; Fiber 1.1 grams

Mr. Keto's Parmesan Garlic Wings

Mr. Keto is the nickname my YouTube subscribers gave my husband when he joined me to make videos of some of his favorite low carb recipes. We've made this for parties and for simple dinners. No matter how many pounds of wings we make, it is never enough.

Video: http://bit.ly/CookingKetoWithKristieParaesanGarlicChickenWings

INGREDIENTS

2 pounds chicken wings/drumettes
2 tablespoons bacon fat
1/4 teaspoon garlic powder
1 tablespoon minced garlic
1/4 teaspoon black pepper

1 tablespoon salt
1/4 teaspoon red pepper flakes (optional)
1/3 cup parmesan cheese

Place chicken in large bowl. Add bacon fat and spices. Mix until all chicken pieces are coated. Marinate in refrigerator for 1/2 hour. Grill (apple wood chips added to smoker) or bake in oven at 425 degrees for 25 to 30 minutes until done. Place cooked chicken in large bowl and add parmesan cheese stirring until coated. Serve warm with homemade Ranch dressing on page 121 or Blue Cheese dressing on page 111.

NUTRITION FACTS 6 servings. Per serving: Calories: 391.2; Fat: 28.9 grams; Protein 28.9 grams; Carbohydrate 0.5 grams; Fiber 0 grams

Baked Fish Sticks

My family isn't fond of seafood, but my children used to eat fish sticks in our high carb heyday. The first time I made these, I worried that they would never touch them. Without saying a word, I simply served them for dinner one night. My very picky son, exclaimed, "Yay, I love fish sticks!" I agreed that they were good fish sticks, and that's how this recipe was named.

INGREDIENTS

1 lb. cod filets, cut in 2 ounce pieces
1 cup pork rind crumbs
1/2 cup fresh parmesan, finely shredded

1/3 cup oat fiber (omit if you don't use oat fiber)
2 eggs, well beaten

Pat the filets with paper towel to remove excess moisture. Prepare two shallow glass dishes, and line a baking sheet with parchment paper. In one dish, mix the "breading" of pork rind crumbs, parmesan, and oat fiber. Blend well. In the second dish, add the well beaten egg. First, dip a cod filet in the egg, turning to coat with egg. Next, dip the filet in the breading, turning to coat with the mix. Lay breaded pieces of cod on a baking sheet. Bake at 350 degrees for 18 to 22 minutes or until filets are lightly browned and tender. Do not overcook. Serve with cole slaw on page 103.

NUTRITION FACTS 2 servings. Per serving: Calories: 78; Fat: 5 grams; Protein 6 grams; Carbohydrate 0.6 grams; Fiber 0 grams

Keto Crab Cakes

I have always loved crab cakes, and while crab is naturally low carb, most restaurants add bread crumbs or other high carb fillers. The bread crumbs serve as a binder, so I replaced them with low carb options that also act as binders. In this recipe, freshly grated parmesan cheese, pork rinds, and an egg hold these together. Fry them in ghee or bacon fat for the best flavor.

INGREDIENTS

- 1 lb. crab meat, shells removed
- 1/4 cup mayonnaise
- 1/2 teaspoon Worcestershire sauce
- 1 egg, beaten
- 1/2 teaspoon dry mustard
- 2 teaspoons dried minced onion
- 1 teaspoon lemon juice
- 1/4 cup pork rinds, crushed into fine powder
- 1 1/2 teaspoon oat fiber (optional)
- 1/4 cup Parmesan cheese, finely grated
- 1/4 teaspoon salt
- 1 teaspoon dried parsley
- 1/8 teaspoon Cayenne pepper or 1 teaspoon Old Bay Seasoning (optional)
- Bacon fat or ghee for frying

Drain crab meat and place in a mixing bowl. Use a fork to check for shells and to separate into smaller pieces. Add next 6 ingredients and mix well. Add remaining ingredients, and stir until thoroughly combined. Let the mixture rest in the refrigerator for 20 to 30 minutes. Shape into 1 1/2 to 2 inch patties. Fry crab cakes on medium high heat for 4 to 6 minutes on each side until lightly browned. Serve with tartar sauce to increase the fat macros.

NUTRITION FACTS
4 servings. Per serving: Calories: 198.8; Fat: 10.6 grams; Protein 19.5 grams; Carbohydrate 0.9 grams; Fiber 0 grams

Photo courtesy of Lori Bartell Weed

Mussels in White Wine Sauce

Cooking mussels for the first time was really intimidating to me, but it was actually very easy. In fact, this is so easy to make that whenever I see fresh mussels on sale I grab a few pounds because it is a very quick meal. If there are leftovers, I remove the mussels from the shells and store them in any leftover sauce and enjoy them for lunch the following day.

INGREDIENTS

2 lbs. fresh mussels, scrubbed and debearded

4 tablespoons butter

1 clove garlic

1/3 cup leek, chopped

1 1/2 cup dry white wine

1/2 cup heavy cream

2 tablespoons fresh parsley, chopped

Salt and pepper to taste

Rinse and scrub mussels with cold water. Use a knife to remove "beards" and discard them. Also discard any mussels that do not close when tapped. In a large pot, melt butter. Add garlic and leek and sauté for 5 to 7 minutes. Add white wine and mussels. Increase heat to high and cover for 5 to 7 minutes. Mussels are done when they open. Discard any mussels that have not opened after 10 to 12 minutes. Uncover and reduce heat. Add heavy cream and fresh parsley. Season with salt and pepper. Serve mussels and sauce over sautéed spinach if desired.

NUTRITION FACTS 4 servings. Per serving: Calories: 409.5; Fat: 15.7 grams; Protein 19 grams; Carbohydrate 6.4 grams; Fiber 0.3 grams

Photo courtesy of Rebecca Scavello

Pan-Seared Scallops

Scallops are simple and sweet and very easy to prepare. This dish is easy to make for guests or for a special occasion. We usually enjoy them over sautéed spinach or with a spinach salad.

INGREDIENTS

1 1/2 lbs. large sea scallops (16 to 20) 1/3 cup white wine
1 tablespoon ghee   1/3 cup finely shredded Parmesan cheese
3 tablespoons butter   3 tablespoons bacon, finely chopped

Rinse scallops and dry well. Place in a single layer on a dry towel and press gently with a second dry towel to remove moisture. In a large skillet, heat ghee on a very high heat. When the skillet is hot, add scallops in a single layer. Sear 1 to 1 1/2 minutes on each side. Do not overcook. Remove scallops from the pan and place in a single layer on a serving dish. Sprinkle bacon pieces and parmesan cheese over the scallops. In the same pan used to cook the scallops, add butter and wine. Simmer 5 to 6 minutes to melt butter and reduce the wine. Use a wooden spoon to scrape the sides of the pan so that any browned bits are added to the sauce. Pour the reduced pan sauce over the scallops and serve immediately.

NUTRITION FACTS 2 servings. Per serving: Calories: 700.1; Fat: 26.7 grams; Protein 81.8 grams; Carbohydrate 3.5 grams; Fiber 0 grams

Photo courtesy of Jan Walinck

Crazy for Carnitas

Carnitas are great for feeding a crowd. You can roast the pork or cook it in a crockpot. Just be sure to follow the final step of browning it in the skillet in some of the roasting juices. The browned bits are where the magic happens. Serve it with bell pepper and onion that have been sautéed in the same pan juices. Don't forget the sour cream, shredded cheese, avocado, and fresh cilantro. I serve it with avocado crema (recipe on page 117).

Video: http://bit.ly/CookingKetoWithKristieCrazyForCarnitas

INGREDIENTS

5 lbs. pork shoulder or Boston butt cut into smaller chunks
Seasoning for meat
2 tablespoons cumin
1 tablespoon chili powder
1 tablespoon garlic powder
2 tablespoons oregano
1 teaspoon salt

1/4 to 1/3 cup jalapenos, fresh or jarred
2 ounces fresh squeezed orange juice OR 1 teaspoon orange extract
1 tablespoon orange zest (just orange part, no white)
2 tablespoons lime juice
Juice of one lemon

Mix spices and rub the spice on the meat. Place the meat fatty side up into a crock pot or oven safe skillet. Sprinkle jalapenos over the meat. Add fresh orange juice, lime juice, and lemon juice. Cook on low in the crock pot for 10 to 12 hours or overnight. When the meat is tender, remove the meat from the crockpot, and shred it into smaller pieces. Reserve the pan drippings. Boil pan drippings down to at least half. Heat a heavy skillet on high heat. Add some of the reduced pan drippings. Fry the pork in a heavy skillet until the pieces are browned and crispy. Getting the meat crisped up is really important in making it so delicious.

Serve with onions, peppers, poblanos, or jalapenos that have been sautéed in some of the pan drippings. Carnitas are best served with fresh avocado, shredded cheese, sour cream, avocado crema, or fresh tomatoes. Don't forget the fresh cilantro!

NUTRITION FACTS 12 servings. Per serving: Calories: 492.8; Fat: 39.6 grams; Protein 33.3 grams; Carbohydrate 1.6 grams; Fiber 0 grams

Carne Asada {Mexican Beef}

When I want everyone home for dinner, I make Carne Asada, a tender beef with mild Tex-Mex spices. This dish is also great to take to a potluck as long as you're willing to share!

INGREDIENTS

3 lbs of beef thinly sliced

2 tablespoons cumin

2 tablespoons chili powder

1 tablespoon paprika

1 tablespoon smoked paprika

1 tablespoon oregano

1 teaspoon salt

1 tablespoon minced garlic

1/3 cup lime juice

1/2 cup avocado oil (or your preferred oil)

Mix dry spices. Reserve three to four tablespoons of dry spice. Mix dry ingredients with garlic, oil, and lime juice to make marinade and pour over meat. Let the meat marinate for 4 to 6 hours or over night.

After the meat has marinated, cook for about 8 hours in a slow cooker or for about 45 minutes in a very large skillet. After browning the meat, cover and let simmer on low for about 45 minutes. Remove the cover to the skillet and let the liquid cook off. In a separate pan, prepare the vegetables.

INGREDIENTS

2 tablespoons avocado oil or bacon fat

1 large onion, sliced

1 large bell pepper, sliced

2 jalapeno peppers, sliced

2 tablespoons spice mix from above

Juice from one lime

Sprinkle of salt

Saute veggies in avocado oil or bacon fat. As the vegetables begin to cook, add spices. Serve with sour cream, avocado (avocado crema), cheese, and low carb salsa.

NUTRITION FACTS 8 servings. Per serving: Calories: 604.6; Fat: 50 grams; Protein 29.9 grams; Carbohydrate 5.7 grams; Fiber 1.3 grams

White Chicken Spinach & Artichoke Lasagna with Bacon Noodles

Bacon noodles? Yes! My white lasagna recipe was inspired by one of the best high carb meals I have ever eaten. While menu planning one day, I came across my old high-carb recipe, and decided that it would fit perfectly in my keto world if I could just use different noodles. I'd never considered bacon before, but as I considered it, I couldn't imagine anything that isn't better with bacon. I'm also smitten with the white sauce in this recipe. It makes a great sauce for any meat or vegetable.

Video: http://bit.ly/CookingKetoWithKristieWhiteLasagne

INGREDIENTS

Veggie Layer
2 tablespoons bacon fat
1/3 cup chopped onion
2 stalks celery chopped

1 cup chopped mushrooms
1 chopped and seeded jalapeno (optional)
1 tablespoon garlic
1 teaspoon salt
1 tablespoon finely chopped Sun-dried tomatoes

Step 1 - Melt the bacon fat in a heavy skillet. Add the onion, celery, mushrooms, jalapeno, garlic, and salt and simmer until veggies are tender and slightly browned.

INGREDIENTS

9 ounces spinach cooked and drained   3/4 cup country ham (optional)
1/2 cup artichoke hearts

Step 2 - Add to the veggie mixture and set aside.

INGREDIENTS

Sauce recipe
4 ounces cream cheese
3 tablespoons Kerrygold butter
1 cup bone broth
1 teaspoon dried parsley (optional)

1 teaspoon garlic
1/4 teaspoon salt
1/2 cup heavy cream
3 teaspoons Worcestershire sauce
1/2 cup sour cream
1/2 teaspoon glucomannan

Step 3 - Melt butter and cream cheese in the bone broth. Add parsley, garlic, Worcestershire sauce, and salt. Whisk at low heat until it simmers. Whisk in sour cream and heavy cream. Keep the heat low so that the sauce doesn't break.

{Lasagna Continued}

INGREDIENTS

3 cups chopped chicken
16 strips of cooked bacon
2 1/2 cups shredded cheese (a blend of asiago, cheddar, Monterey jack, or gouda work well. Gouda and asiago are my favorite)
1 cup of parmesan cheese or a parmesan cheese blend

Step 4 - In a 9" by 13" glass baking dish, start with a layer chicken; add a layer of veggies including artichoke hearts and spinach. Top with a little less than half of the white sauce. Add a layer of shredded cheese—use your favorite. Use cooked bacon as a "noodle" layer. Repeat layers of chicken, veggies, bacon, cheese, and sauce. Bake at 375 degrees for about 30 to 35 minutes until everything is bubbly and hot. During the last 5 minutes cover the lasagna with the Parmesan blend. Let cool at least 5 minutes before serving.

NUTRITION FACTS 12 servings. Per serving: Calories: 400.4; Fat: 30.6 grams; Protein 32.4 grams; Carbohydrate 5.2 grams; Fiber 1.2 grams

Sandy's Picadillo {Shredded Beef}

Sandy Amaya is a low carb friend from Arizona who was very generous to share her authentic recipe with me. The first time I made this we used video conferencing to cook together, and it was hilarious! Sandy is an excellent cook, and I'm so grateful that she shared her recipe with me so that I can share it with you.
Video: http://bit.ly/CookingKetoWithKristiePicadillo

INGREDIENTS

Shredded Beef
1.5 lbs. beef, thinly sliced or shredded chuck roast
1 teaspoon salt

1/4 teaspoon pepper
1 clove garlic
1/3 cup water

Cook the beef in the water with the seasonings until the water cooks out and the meat is browned and tender. While the beef cooks, make the Chile sauce.

Chile Sauce
7 tomatillos, husked and rinsed
1/4 small onion
3 large jalapenos (seed them and use fewer for a less spicy flavor)

1 clove garlic
1 tablespoon fresh cilantro
1/3 cup water (may need to add a bit more)
1/2 teaspoon salt

Add water to cover the veggies. Bring to a boil until the tomatillos and jalapenos soften, about 10 to 15 minutes. The jalapenos will change to an army green color. Strain the vegetables and puree them in a blender or Ninja. Remove the seeds from the jalapenos if you want a milder sauce. Add 1/3 cup or so of water to thin the Chile sauce. Blend well and set aside.

Vegetables
1 tablespoon bacon fat
1 Roma tomato, chopped
1 small onion, chopped
1 jalapeno, seeded and chopped
1/2 clove garlic, crushed

Sautee vegetables until just crisp tender. Add the shredded beef. Lower the heat, and let simmer with the vegetables. When the vegetables are tender, add the Chile sauce to the beef and vegetable mix. Let the entire mixture simmer for 5 to 10 minutes. Serve with queso fresco and more fresh cilantro and avocado, if desired.

NUTRITION FACTS 6 servings. Per serving: Calories: 328.4; Fat: 24.4 grams; Protein 20.1 grams; Carbohydrate 6.8 grams; Fiber 2.1 grams

Spinach Salad with Grandmother's Hot Bacon Fat Vinaigrette

The spinach, eggs, bacon, and parmesan salad are okay, but let's be honest. It's the Hot Bacon Fat Dressing on page 120 that makes this one of my best recipes. You can add meat to this salad to increase the protein, and you can use your favorite homemade salad dressing, but until you try Grandmother's Hot Bacon Fat Dressing on this salad, then you haven't made this recipe!

INGREDIENTS

6 cups fresh spinach

2 hard-boiled eggs, chopped

1/2 cup bacon pieces

1/3 cup Parmesan, finely grated (optional)

Wash spinach and remove tough ends. Dry leaves. Divide spinach evenly among four salad plates. Top with hard-boiled eggs and bacon divided evenly among the plates. Sprinkle on Parmesan cheese if desired. Dress with hot bacon fat dressing (recipe on page 120), and serve immediately.

NUTRITION FACTS 4 servings. Per serving: Calories: 203.8; Fat: 6.8 grams; Protein 12.9 grams; Carbohydrate 2.1 grams; Fiber 1.2 grams

Simple Chicken Salad

My simple chicken salad is one of my favorite lunches. I can also toss it together quickly for a summer meal or to share at a potluck. All of the ingredients are easy to find and inexpensive, which puts this recipe near the top of my list.

INGREDIENTS

2 cups cooked chicken, shredded

1/2 cup mayonnaise

2 tablespoons chopped dill pickles

2 tablespoons bacon pieces

1 teaspoon dry mustard

2 drops liquid sweetener (optional)

Salt and pepper to taste

1 hard-boiled egg, finely chopped (optional)

Mix the mayonnaise, pickles, mustard, sweetener, salt, and pepper. Toss in the shredded chicken, bacon, and egg. Mix all ingredients well. Refrigerate for thirty minutes before serving.

NUTRITION FACTS 4 servings. Per serving: Calories: 298.8; Fat: 22.5 grams; Protein 24.5 grams; Carbohydrate 0.4 grams; Fiber 0 grams

Cold Salmon Salad

Wild caught salmon adds omega 3 that our bodies seem to need. This cold salad adds additional fats that balance the fat and protein macros and packs a lot of flavor. The cucumber gives it a great texture as well. This is another frequent lunch option for me to make ahead of time or a quick dinner if I haven't planned ahead.

INGREDIENTS

14.75 ounce Trader Joe's canned salmon

1 teaspoon dried dill weed

1/3 cup mayonnaise

1 1/2 tablespoon lemon juice

1 teaspoon Dijon mustard

1/3 cup English cucumber, peeled and chopped

1 teaspoon garlic powder

2 tablespoon celery, finely chopped (optional)

1/2 teaspoon salt

1/4 teaspoon white pepper

Mix mayonnaise, dill, lemon juice, mustard, garlic, salt and pepper. Add salmon, cucumber, and celery and mix until well combined. Delicious served over fresh spinach or chopped Romaine lettuce.

NUTRITION FACTS 2 servings. Per serving: Calories: 523.5; Fat: 41.5 grams; Protein 42 grams; Carbohydrate 1.3 grams; Fiber 0.3 grams

Photo courtesy of Carol Turpen Pitts

Egg Salad with Bacon

My mother always made the best egg salad, until I discovered that adding a little cream cheese, bacon, and green onion made it even better. This is her recipe with my keto modifications. I enjoy with a couple of stalks of celery or my favorite pork rinds.

INGREDIENTS
6 boiled eggs, finely chopped
1/3 cup mayonnaise
1 1/2 teaspoons prepared mustard
2 ounces cream cheese, softened
1 green onion tops, finely chopped (optional)

1/4 teaspoon salt
1/4 teaspoon pepper
2 tablespoons bacon pieces

Mix softened cream cheese, mayonnaise, mustard, salt, and pepper. Add bacon, eggs, green onion, and mix until well combined. Serve chilled.

NUTRITION FACTS
2 servings. Per serving: Calories: 494; Fat: 43.5 grams; Protein 22 grams; Carbohydrate 2.8 grams; Fiber 0 grams

Photo courtesy of Kirk Pullen Photography

Chapter 3

SATISFYING SIDES

Most traditional meals focus on a meat and two vegetables. We are taught "5 a day" fruits and vegetables and that mantra shapes how many of us meal plan. When my family transitioned to low carb high fat, I had to rethink that notion since most vegetables are primarily carbohydrates and provide little, if any, fat and protein. In contrast to our pre-lchf meals, our current meals tend to feature a main dish which is usually a meat and just one side in order to control the number of carbohydrates in a meal. Just as with any recipe, please calculate the nutritional information with the ingredients that you use. Also, to minimize carb creep, please pay attention to portion size, especially if you're new to lchf. Please also remember that a low carb vegetable is not a "free" food. One serving of cauliflower might be low carb, but two servings is too many for many of us.

As I considered what sides to include in this cookbook, I focused on side dishes that are higher fat and that minimize the carbohydrates by limiting vegetable portions. You will notice that the fat grams per serving are generally very high. I also included recipes that use fairly common or simple ingredients. Each of these recipes are dishes that I not only serve my family, but that I can also share with carbivore friends and family members without their feeling as if this is "diet" food. In fact, unless I mention it, they enjoy these dishes as simple, but delicious sides paired with a protein.

In this section, I've included casseroles that will stand up to any Baptist church homecoming or any southern "dinner on the grounds". Speaking of southern, there's a tomato pie recipe that would make even my grandmother proud. For those who don't love a good casserole there are recipes for simple roasted or sautéed vegetables. Using bacon fat is key.

Some of these sides make great party foods like jalapeno poppers or stuffed mushrooms. You will also be proud to show up at any picnic with low carb faux-tato salad, marinated mushrooms, or 7-layer salad, all tweaked to be as low carb and flavorful as possible. Last, there's a North Carolina red slaw and an "everybody else" white slaw that's perfect for any BBQ or pig-pickin'. Just be sure to take the cookbook with you because everyone there is going to want the recipe!

Creamed Cauli Mash

This is one of the very first keto side dishes I ever made. I still remember the smile on my daughter's face as she asked, "Is this potato?" Nope. It's better than potatoes. Cauli mash is an excellent option to replace creamed potatoes, but please consider portions and carb count. Cauliflower is low carb, but not "no carb", and pureed cauli means the carbohydrates are more concentrated. Still, you can enjoy cauli mash with low carb meatloaf whenever you want.

Video: http://bit.ly/CookingKetoWithKrisiteCauliflowerRecipes

INGREDIENTS

3 cups cauliflower, chopped
4 ounces of butter, softened
1/3 cup heavy cream
2 ounces cream cheese or Havarti or
your favorite creamy cheese

2 ounces sharp cheddar cheese, shredded
(Cabot is my favorite)
1/4 teaspoon garlic powder
1/4 teaspoon salt

First, chop the cauliflower into florets. To "steam" the cauliflower, use a microwave safe dish. Do not add any water or moisture. Microwave the cauliflower for 4 to 5 minutes or until soft. Use a clean hand towel or paper towel to squeeze moisture from the steamed cauliflower. Transfer the steamed cauli to a blender. Add butter, heavy cream, cheeses, garlic powder, and salt. Blend until mixture is pureed and creamy. After pureeing the mixture, you may want to warm it before serving.

NUTRITION FACTS 6 servings. Per serving: Calories: 292; Fat: 21.5 grams; Protein 5.6 grams; Carbohydrate 3.7 grams; Fiber 1.3 grams

Twice-Baked Cauliflower Casserole

Consider the plain, low-fat potato. What makes it taste good? It's the butter, bacon, sour cream, and salt that bring the flavor. Fortunately those good tastes are all keto-friendly and so is cauliflower. Twice-baked Cauliflower Casserole is one of those dishes that I take to large gatherings to share with others, and it is always a hit even with the carbivores.

Video: http://bit.ly/CookingKetoWithKrisiteCauliflowerRecipes

INGREDIENTS

4 cups steamed cauliflower, chopped
1/2 cup bacon pieces
3 ounces butter, softened
1/2 cup sour cream
4 ounces of cream cheese

1/4 teaspoon garlic powder
Fresh cracked pepper
1/4 teaspoon salt
1/2 tablespoon dehydrated onion
1 1/2 cup cheddar cheese, shredded

Cut cauliflower into small, bite-sized pieces and place in a microwave safe glass dish. Microwave on high for 4 to 6 minutes or until tender, but not mushy. In a mixing bowl, mix steamed, chopped cauli, bacon, butter, sour cream, and cream cheese. Mix well. Add garlic powder, salt (omit if using salted butter), fresh pepper, and dehydrated onion and mix until incorporated. Stir in cheddar cheese. Pour mixture into a 9" by 13" glass baking dish. Bake at 350 degrees for about 25 to 30 minutes or until browned and bubbly.

NUTRITION FACTS 8 servings. Per serving: Calories: 263.1; Fat: 22.1 grams; Protein 10.8 grams; Carbohydrate 4.2 grams; Fiber 1.1 grams

Photo courtesy of Kat Macie

Creamed Spinach

Creamed Spinach is a staple for busy weeknight meals because it can be made quickly, and it uses ingredients that I nearly always have on hand. Moreover, there's only a skillet to clean afterwards and that is always a bonus here!

INGREDIENTS

12 ounce package of bagged spinach
1 tablespoon bacon fat (or butter or ghee)
1 teaspoon dried minced onion
2 tablespoons butter

2 ounces cream cheese, cubed and softened
1/3 cup heavy cream OR 1/4 cup heavy cream and 2 tablespoons broth
1/4 teaspoon garlic powder
1/4 cup parmesan, grated

In a large skillet on medium heat, melt the bacon fat. Add spinach to the skillet by handfuls. Use a spoon or tongs to stir the spinach as you add more. Add the onion and butter. As soon as the spinach has just wilted and cooked down, push the spinach to the side to create a place to add the cream cheese and heavy cream. Stir the cream cheese and cream until melted. Add the garlic powder and stir until the cream cheese and heavy cream are distributed throughout the spinach. Top with 1/4 cup freshly grated parmesan just before serving.

NUTRITION FACTS 4 servings. Per serving: Calories: 255.3; Fat: 14.2 grams; Protein 2.3 grams; Carbohydrate 2.4 grams; Fiber 0.7 grams

Broccoli Casserole

Broccoli casserole was one of the first casseroles that I ever made. Once, when I was much younger, I was having friends visit my first new home. I was really excited to cook for them, but decided to take a shortcut and didn't cook the broccoli. Instead, I tossed it into the casserole raw. When we sat down to eat, the broccoli was still crunchy and tasted raw. It was awful! I've learned a few things about cooking since then, and one of them is to always, always, steam the broccoli. This recipe is just like my high carb favorite, except it uses pork rinds instead of bread crumbs. I now make this version for family and friends. You can also add chicken or sausage to this casserole for a complete and hearty meal.

INGREDIENTS

4 cups broccoli, steamed
1/3 cup finely chopped onion
2 tablespoons butter, melted
1/4 teaspoon freshly ground pepper

1/2 cup mayonnaise
1/2 cup full fat sour cream
1 1/2 cup cheddar cheese, shredded
3/4 cup pork rind dust (ground pork rinds)

Cut the broccoli into bite-sized pieces and steam until tender. Drain well and let cool. Set aside. In a large mixing bowl, mix mayonnaise, sour cream, onion, butter, and pepper. Add cheese, pork rind dust, and broccoli. Mix well and pour into a casserole dish. Bake at 350 degrees until browned and bubbly, about 25 minutes.

NUTRITION FACTS 8 servings. Per serving: Calories: 275.6; Fat: 24 grams; Protein 11.6 grams; Carbohydrate 4.4 grams; Fiber 1.3 grams

Broccoli Salad

Sometimes the simplest dishes made from common ingredients are the best. Broccoli salad is one of those recipes that is easy to make quickly, but will get lots of compliments. This is another one that is a great a dish to share and easy enough to make for busy weeknight meals.

Video: http://bit.ly/CookingKetoWithKristieBroccoliSalad

INGREDIENTS
4 cups of raw broccoli florets (small pieces like the tip of your baby finger)
1/4 cup finely chopped onion
1/2 cup bacon, chopped
1 1/2 cup of cheddar cheese

Dressing
1 cup of mayonnaise
1 1/2 tablespoons of apple cider vinegar
2 tablespoon granulated sweetener or 6 drops liquid sweetener
salt
pepper

In a large bowl, toss together the broccoli, onion, bacon, and cheese. In a small mixing bowl, mix together the mayonnaise, vinegar, sweetener, salt, and pepper. Pour the dressing over the broccoli mixture and toss well to combine. Refrigerate for at least 30 minutes before serving.

NUTRITION FACTS 8 servings. Per serving: Calories: 275.1; Fat: 26.4 grams; Protein 9.6 grams; Carbohydrate 3.6 grams; Fiber 1.3 grams

Photo courtesy of Davita Blevins and Whitney Martin

Loaded Roasted Broccoli

Think of a loaded baked potato—creamy sour cream, bacon pieces, and shredded cheddar—melty and fatty and wonderful! Now, remove the potato since it doesn't have any flavor anyway, and replace it with roasted broccoli. That's what she said! Tip: In restaurants that serve loaded baked potatoes, ask for this as a side using broccoli instead of a potato.

INGREDIENTS

4 cups broccoli florets, roasted

1/2 cup sour cream

1/2 cup cheddar cheese, shredded

1/2 cup bacon pieces

Cut the broccoli into long, but thinner florets. In a large bowl, toss the broccoli with a tablespoon of melted bacon fat until lightly coated. To roast the broccoli, spread the pieces on a large baking sheet that has been covered with foil. Roast at 375 degrees for 12 to 16 minutes or until lightly browned. Place the broccoli on a serving dish and cover with grated cheese while still warm. Sprinkle the bacon over the cheese. Add dollops of sour cream over the top. Serve immediately. You can also use steamed broccoli, but roasting it adds incredible flavor to this dish.

NUTRITION FACTS 8 servings. Per serving: Calories: 98; Fat: 6.4 grams; Protein 6.5 grams; Carbohydrate 3.7 grams; Fiber 1.2 grams

Fried Creamed Cabbage

Cabbage is one of those vegetables that doesn't get a lot of attention, but it is inexpensive and very versatile. We enjoy it raw in salads or in slaws. When cooked, it absorbs some of the fat and becomes a great low carb vegetable option. You can also slice it and cook it to have a noodle replacement. In this dish, the cabbage provides a great base for a creamy sauce with bacon and Parmesan. Add a simple protein and this is a very good and inexpensive meal.

Video: http://bit.ly/CookingKetoWithKristieCabbageSkillet

INGREDIENTS

1/2 cup pancetta (or bacon)
1 teaspoon fresh garlic
3 cups cabbage, chopped
2 tablespoons bacon fat or ghee
1/4 cup onion, chopped (optional)
1/4 cup bacon, chopped (optional)

Sea salt to taste
Pepper to taste
2 ounces cream cheese
1/3 cup sour cream
2 tablespoons heavy cream
1/3 cup grated parmesan (or mild cheese of choice)

On medium heat, pan fry the pancetta until brown. Add garlic, cabbage, onion and bacon fat. Sauté until the cabbage is tender, which takes about 10 minutes. Add bacon, salt and pepper to taste. Turn heat to low so that the dairy doesn't separate or break. Push fried cabbage to one side of the pan. In the open space, add sour cream and cream cheese, stirring until melted. Blend into the cabbage and add heavy cream. Stir until creamy and smooth. If the cream is too thick add a little chicken broth to thin. Sprinkle parmesan cheese over top before serving.

NUTRITION FACTS
6 servings. Per serving: Calories: 261.6; Fat: 21.1 grams; Protein 11.6 grams; Carbohydrate 4.1 grams; Fiber 1.1 grams

Sauteed Spaghetti Squash

Spaghetti squash is a fickle friend with whom you should take great care. First, at 7 carbs per cup, you need to be aware of serving size. Second, if spaghetti squash is overcooked, it takes on a sweet taste. When I used to roast spaghetti squash in the oven, I was always disappointed in the sweetness since I wanted to use it in savory dishes. When I began cooking it in the microwave, I used less cooking time and the squash no longer tasted as sweet. Be sure to pierce the skin of the squash with a sharp knife before microwaving or it can explode. Also, you can prep this dish ahead of time by cooking the spaghetti squash on the weekend, scraping out the inside, and waiting to sauté it just before serving.

INGREDIENTS

4 cups spaghetti squash	1/4 teaspoon salt
6 tablespoons butter	1 teaspoon dried parsley flakes
1 teaspoon fresh garlic	1/3 cup parmesan cheese, grated (optional)

Use a sharp knife to pierce the outside skin of the spaghetti squash. Microwave on high power for 7 to 8 minutes, depending on the size of the spaghetti squash. You will know it has cooked long enough when it yields to gentle pressure. Let sit at least 15 minutes or until cool enough to touch. When cooled, slice in half. Use a spoon to gently scoop out the seeds. When the seeds are removed, use a fork to scrape the inside of the spaghetti squash into a bowl. Measure out 3 cups of spaghetti squash and set the remainder aside.

In a large skillet, heat the butter on medium low heat. Add the spaghetti squash and the garlic and cook on low heat for 6 to 8 minutes or until it dries out a little. Season with salt and parsley. When the squash is tender, increase the heat to medium heat. Continue stirring as the squash browns slightly. Pour into a serving bowl and top with crumbled bacon if desired.

NUTRITION FACTS
8 servings. Per serving: Calories: 106.4; Fat: 9.1 grams; Protein 1.5 grams; Carbohydrate 3.6 grams; Fiber 0 grams

Old Fashioned Baked Mac N Cheese

I used to make a high carb version of this that my family and friends adored. I made a double batch so there would be "enough". There's probably remnants of it on my hips today! This version won't "stick around" in your pots or on your thighs. The Miracle noodle brand shirataki noodles that I use for this low carb version are made from konjac, which has no impact on blood glucose. After baking, they have a slightly soft texture like traditional noodles. I avoid the low carb noodles made from soy, so I do not recommend those. If you don't have Miracle noodles or don't like them, you can use zoodles (zucchini noodles). Just let them dry out by spiralizing them and laying them out for several hours. Do not cook them in advance.

INGREDIENTS

3 packages of shirataki fettucine noodles, cut into 1 inch lengths
2 cups of shredded sharp cheddar cheese (8 ounces)
2 cups of shredded mild cheddar cheese (8 ounces)
3 ounces cream cheese
5 ounces butter
1 cup heavy cream
1/2 cup sour cream

2 eggs, well beaten
1 teaspoon salt
1/2 teaspoon garlic
1/4 teaspoon cayenne pepper (optional)

Topping
1/3 cup pork rind dust
1/3 cup parmesan cheese
1/4 cup oat fiber
2 1/2 tablespoons butter

If you are using Miracle brand or konjac noodles, rinse thoroughly (several minutes) under cold water. If you are using zuchinni noodles, spiralize them and set aside to dry out.

In a large sauce pan, use low heat to melt the cream cheese and butter. When melted, use a whisk to stir in the heavy cream, sour cream, and eggs. Use a low heat so that the cream does not break. Mix until creamy and smooth. Add salt, garlic, and cayenne pepper. Remove from heat and stir in the "noodles" and shredded cheeses.

Pour the mixture into a greased 9" by 13" glass baking dish. Mix the pork rind dust, parmesan cheese, oat fiber, and butter. It should be coarse like sand. Sprinkle the mixture over the top of the noodle mix. Bake for 25 to 30 minutes at 325 degrees until golden brown and bubbling. Let cool for 10 minutes before serving.

NUTRITION FACTS 8 servings. Per serving: Calories: 499.4; Fat: 47 grams; Protein 17.8 grams; Carbohydrate 3.1 grams; Fiber 0 grams

Southern Summer Tomato Pie

The summer before I went low carb I discovered tomato pie. It had been love at first bite. Two years later, I had tomato pie on my mind when I started thinking about what was in tomato pie. I knew that tomatoes were carby, and that I would have to limit the amount I used, but I also how to make some pretty good savory crusts and I figured that just maybe..... After a little of this and a pinch of that, and a few prayers and maybe a few cusses, I had my favorite summer pie! This Tomato Pie is something special and worth every single carb.

INGREDIENTS

Crust

3/4 cup almond flour
1/3 cup oat fiber (or 2 tablespoons coconut flour)
1 cup shredded parmesan cheese
1 egg
1/4 teaspoon salt
2 tablespoons bacon fat (or coconut oil, ghee, or butter)

Filling

5 large tomatoes, peeled and sliced
1/2 cup mayonnaise
1/3 cup chopped bacon or real bacon pieces
1 cup shredded cheese
1/3 cup finely slivered onion

Mix parmesan cheese, almond flour, oat fiber, egg, bacon fat, and salt. Press into a 9" pie plate, being sure to press the crust up the sides. When the crust is prepared, bake for 15 minutes at 350 degrees and allow to cool.

Place sliced tomatoes over the cooled crust. The slices should cover the crust and will be about two slices deep. Sprinkle bacon pieces over tomato slices and add onion slices. In a separate bowl, mix the mayonnaise and cheese together. Spread the mayonnaise mixture over the sliced tomatoes. Spread the mixture to the edges of the crust to "seal" the toppings. Sprinkle dried oregano and dried basil over the top. Bake at 350 degrees for about 30 minutes. The topping will be browned and bubbly when done. Let set for at least 10 minutes before serving. Enjoy warm or cold.

NUTRITION FACTS 12 servings. Per serving: Calories: 198; Fat: 15.8 grams; Protein 8.4 grams; Carbohydrate 4.8 grams; Fiber 1.8 grams

Marinated Mushrooms

Mushrooms are naturally lower carb and marinating them in good fats makes them that much more keto-friendly. These mushrooms seem to absorb more of the fat and flavor because they are boiled first and then marinated. You can serve this as part of an anti-pasta platter, warm them to serve as a side dish, or slice them up to top a fathead pizza.

INGREDIENTS

1 lb. mushrooms, cleaned
1 1/2 cup apple cider vinegar, divided
1 1/2 cup water
3 cloves garlic, crushed
1/2 small onion, sliced
1/2 cup olive oil

2 teaspoons salt
2 teaspoons dried parsley
1 teaspoon oregano
1 tablespoon Italian seasonings
4 drops liquid sweetener (optional)
1/4 teaspoons red pepper (optional)

Add water and 1 cup of the apple cider vinegar to a large pot. Add the cleaned mushrooms, slicing larger mushrooms in half if desired. Boil for 5 minutes. Drain well. Use a clean towel to squeeze the excess moisture from the mushrooms. Place the mushrooms in a gallon-sized freezer bag or a large glass jar. Set aside. In a separate bowl, mix the remaining 1/2 cup apple cider vinegar, olive oil, garlic, onion, salt, parsley, oregano, Italian seasonings, sweetener, and red pepper. Pour the marinade over the dried mushrooms, making sure to coat each one. Place the mushrooms in a refrigerator and let marinate at least 12 to 24 hours before serving.

NUTRITION FACTS 8 servings. Per serving: Calories: 138; Fat: 14.4 grams; Protein 2.0 grams; Carbohydrate 3.1 grams; Fiber 0.8 grams

Stuffed Mushrooms

Adding sausage to this stuffed mushroom recipe makes it hard to resist. These are great as a side or on a party table for you and your carnivore friends. It's nice to have foods like this to share that seem commonplace and not like "diet" food. For a special treat use brie instead of cheddar cheese.

INGREDIENTS

16-ounce package of mushrooms

3/4 lb. Italian sausage, cooked and crumbled

6 ounces cream cheese, softened

1 1/4 cup sharp cheddar, shredded

1 teaspoon dried chives or 1 green onion finely chopped

1/4 teaspoon garlic powder

Use a paper towel to clean the mushrooms. Next, remove the mushroom stems, leaving only the caps. Set aside. In a mixing bowl, mix the cream cheese, sausage, cheese, chives, and garlic powder. When well mixed, use a large spoon to stuff the mushroom caps. The back of the spoon is perfect for pressing the filling into the mushroom. Place mushrooms in a single layer on a baking sheet lined with foil. Bake at 350 degrees for 10 to 12 minutes. Mushrooms should be tender and the filling should be bubbly and brown. Do not over fill the mushroom caps. Serve warm.

NUTRITION FACTS 8 servings. Per serving: Calories: 425; Fat: 22.9 grams; Protein 12.9 grams; Carbohydrate 2 grams; Fiber 0.5 grams

Roasted Brussels Sprouts

No mushy Brussels spouts in our keto family! Even if you've never been a fan of Brussels sprouts, roasting them gives them a deep, earthy flavor you might actually enjoy. The blackened pieces are my favorite.

INGREDIENTS
2 cups Brussels sprouts, chopped or quartered   1/2 teaspoon salt
1 tablespoon bacon fat   1/2 teaspoon cracked black pepper

Wash Brussels sprouts, and chop or quarter them. In a large bowl, toss sprouts with melted bacon fat, salt, and pepper. Spread sprouts into a single over a large baking sheet lined with foil. Roast at 375 degrees for 12 to 16 minutes. Baking time will depend on the size of Brussels sprouts. Stir the sprouts after the first 10 minutes. The sprouts are done when tender and lightly blackened. Serve warm.

NUTRITION FACTS
4 servings. Per serving: Calories: 47.3; Fat: 3.2 grams; Protein 1.5 grams; Carbohydrate 4 grams; Fiber 1.7 grams

Photo courtesy of Kit Schroder

Roasted Crisp Okra

Unfortunately, my family has always loved the heavily breaded and deep fried okra popular in restaurants around the South. We never ate it boiled, but always ate it floured and fried. When family offered us fresh okra from the garden, I decided to try roasting it. Adding the mix of parmesan and pork rind dust give it just a bit of crunch and roasting okra actually gives it even better flavor.

INGREDIENTS

3 cups okra pods (300 grams)
1 tablespoon bacon fat
1/3 cup crushed pork rind dust

1/4 cup finely shredded parmesan cheese
1/2 teaspoon cracked black pepper

Wash okra and pat dry with paper towel. Remove the ends. Slice each pod in half lengthwise. In a large bowl, toss the sliced okra with melted bacon fat. When coated, toss in pork rind dust, parmesan cheese, and pepper. Spread the okra into a single over a large baking sheet lined with foil. Bake at 350 degrees for 15 to 18 minutes. The okra is done when tender and browned.

NUTRITION FACTS 6 servings. Per serving: Calories: 84.7; Fat: 4.3 grams; Protein 5 grams; Carbohydrate 3.6 grams; Fiber 1.5 grams

Loaded Radish Hash

Apart from small slivers of radish in restaurant salads, I had never really eaten them until recently. Only in the past year have I begun to experiment with radishes as a potato substitute, and is a new favorite. Loaded Radish Hash is one of those dishes that you will wonder why you didn't try sooner. It is simple, but be sure to cook the radishes until they are browned and tender.

INGREDIENTS

1 lb radishes, shredded like matchsticks
1 1/2 tablespoons bacon fat
1/4 cup chicken broth
2 tablespoons butter

1/2 cup bacon pieces
2 green onion tops, finely chopped
1 cup sharp cheddar cheese, shredded
1/2 cup sour cream

Clean the radishes and chop off the tops and bottoms. Use a food processor or mandolin to shred the radishes. You want them chopped like matchsticks. Use paper towel to blot out the moisture. In a large skillet, heat the bacon fat. Add the radishes and cook on medium high heat. Fry the radishes until tender and slightly brown. Depending on the size of the pan and thickness of radishes, you may need to reduce heat and cover the skillet with a lid. If the radishes become dry, add 1 tablespoon at a time of chicken broth to add moisture. When radishes are tender, stir in the butter and brown the radishes. After the radish is browned, add the bacon pieces and green onions. Remove from heat and sprinkle the cheese over top. Dollop with sour cream just before serving.

NUTRITION FACTS 6 servings. Per serving: Calories: 221.2; Fat: 18.1 grams; Protein 9.8 grams; Carbohydrate 3.4 grams; Fiber 1.2 grams

Photo courtesy of Kit Schroder

Kristie's Southern Style Pimento Cheese

Pimento Cheese is a true southern delicacy. I grew up eating it on white bread, crusts removed. Thankfully, I learned that the bread is completely unnecessary as this pimento cheese is best eaten from a spoon. You can enjoy it cold with celery or pepperoni chips, or enjoy it as a delicious hot and gooey baked dip. If you aren't yet convinced, just try a dollop over a hot and juicy hamburger.

Video: http://bit.ly/CookingKetoWithKristiePimentoCheese

INGREDIENTS

1 cup plus 1 tablespoon of mayonnaise

2 ounces of cream cheese, softened

16 ounces of shredded cheese (two different cheddars work best)

2 1/2 tablespoons of diced pimentos

1 tablespoon Worcestershire

1/4 teaspoon garlic powder

1/4 teaspoon cayenne powder

5 tablespoons bacon pieces

Mix mayonnaise and cream cheese until well blended. Add the mayonnaise mixture to the shredded cheese and mix well. Add Worcestershire, garlic powder, cayenne, and bacon and blend. Refrigerate for an hour or more before serving.

NUTRITION FACTS 6 servings. Per serving: Calories: 556.2; Fat: 53.9 grams; Protein 21.9 grams; Carbohydrate 0.9 grams; Fiber 0.1 grams

Jalapeno Poppers

Use this yummy filling to stuff jalapenos, mini bell peppers or even mushrooms. We keep it simple with 3 basic ingredients, but you can add browned sausage or even shredded chicken for a heartier appetizer.
Video: http://bit.ly/CookingKetoWithKristieJalapenoPepperPoppers

INGREDIENTS

8 ounces of cream cheese, softened

1 cup bacon piecs

2 1/2 cups shredded cheddar cheese

16 jalapenos washed, sliced into halves, and seeded

Rinse the jalapenos while whole. Slice each in half lengthwise and remove the seeds and white membranes. Dip each half in a bowl of water to remove the seeds. Set aside to dry. Mix the cream cheese, bacon, and shredded cheddar. Fill each jalapeno half with the mixture. Lay the filled jalapeno halves on a baking sheet in a single layer. Bake at 350 degrees until each is browned and tender. Serve immediately.

NUTRITION FACTS 8 servings. Per serving: Calories: 32; Fat: 68.6 grams; Protein 4.8 grams; Carbohydrate 0.9 grams; Fiber 0.3 grams

Jalapeno Popper Deviled Eggs

My husband was hesitant to try these because he does not like deviled eggs. Maybe it was the jalapenos fried in bacon fat, or maybe it was the bacon, or maybe it was that I asked him while videotaping the recipe, but he agreed to try one, and he now has a new favorite side dish.

Video: http://bit.ly/CookingKetoWithKristieJalapenoPepperDeviledEggs

INGREDIENTS

1 dozen hard-boiled eggs, split and yolks removed

2 ounces cream cheese, room temperature

1/2 cup mayonnaise

1 tablespoon prepared mustard

1/4 teaspoon salt

5 tablespoons bacon pieces

2 jalapenos, seeded and sautéed in bacon fat

2 tablespoons bacon fat to sauté the jalapenos

paprika to sprinkle over finished eggs (optional)

Boil 1 dozen eggs. Peel off the shells and split them in half length-wise. Scoop the yolks into a medium sized bowl and set the whites aside. To the egg yolks, add 2 ounces of softened cream cheese, 1/2 cup of mayonnaise, and prepared mustard. Mix all of the ingredients until creamy and well mixed. Add salt, bacon, and jalapenos and mix well. Be sure to add any bacon fat from the pan used to sauté the jalapenos. Fill each egg white half with the mixture. Sprinkle the tops with paprika before serving.

NUTRITION FACTS 6 servings. Per serving: Calories: 324.2; Fat: 28.1 grams; Protein 15.8 grams; Carbohydrate 1.9 grams; Fiber 0.2 grams

Faux-Tato Salad

My mother's signature dish has always been potato salad. She makes it for nearly every holiday and any gathering in between. I've always enjoyed it, but it isn't low carb. When I decided to use cauli as a substitute for potatoes, I called and asked for her potato salad recipe. This is it, except for the potatoes. My doubting husband, who really likes her potato salad, took the first bite and said, "How did you do that?" That's when you know you got it right!

Video: http://bit.ly/CookingKetoWithKristieFauxTatoSalad

INGREDIENTS

3 cups cauliflower, chopped

1 cup of mayonnaise

1/3 cup bell pepper, chopped

1/4 cup finely chopped onion

2 tablespoons chopped dill pickles

1 tablespoon mustard

2 drops liquid sweetener (optional)

Sprinkle of paprika

Cut cauliflower into bite-sized pieces. In a glass dish, microwave the cauliflower for 3 to 4 minutes or until tender, but not soft. While the cauliflower is still warm, add bell pepper, onion, and pickles and mix well. Add the mustard and mayonnaise and stir. Add liquid sweetener, if desired. Mix thoroughly and pour into a serving bowl. May serve warm or chilled. Sprinkle lightly with paprika before serving.

NUTRITION FACTS 6 servings. Per serving: Calories: 217.8; Fat: 24.1 grams; Protein 1.1 grams; Carbohydrate 3.8 grams; Fiber 1.4 grams

Photo courtesy of Carol Turpen Pitts

Seven Layer Salad

A popular potluck dish, Seven Layer Salad traditionally uses English peas and higher carb vegetables. This version includes layers of meats and eggs and fits perfectly with a low carb lifestyle.

INGREDIENTS

3 cups Romaine lettuce, shredded

1 lb sliced turkey

1 1/2 cups cauliflower, chopped into small pieces

1/3 cup onion, finely chopped

6 hard-boiled eggs, chopped or sliced

1 lb cooked bacon, chopped

12 ounces cheddar cheese, shredded

1 cup mayonnaise

1/2 cup sour cream (or crème fraiche)

4 drops liquid sweetener (optional)

1 1/2 tablespoons apple cider vinegar

1/3 cup finely grated Parmesan cheese.

Use a large glass bowl to layer the first seven ingredients. Be sure to put the layers against the edges of the bowl so that the layers can be seen from the outside. Set aside. In another small bowl, mix the mayonnaise, sour cream, sweetener, and vinegar. Spread the mayonnaise over the top of the last layer, smoothing into a solid layer and reaching to the edges of the bowl so that the dressing seals all of the edges. Sprinkle the Parmesan cheese over the top of the dressing. If desired, sprinkle more bacon over the top as a garnish. Because bacon.

NUTRITION FACTS 8 servings. Per serving: Calories: 579; Fat: 47 grams; Protein 36.5 grams; Carbohydrate 3.0 grams; Fiber 0.9 grams

Photo courtesy of Carol Turpen Pitts

Chopped Caprese Salad

Grace and I love this salad. We grow fresh basil each summer just so that we can have Caprese salad on demand. This simple salad has enough fat to accompany nearly any meat or seafood of your choice.

INGREDIENTS

12 ounce ball of fresh mozzarella cheese, chopped

12 grape tomatoes, chopped

2 dozen fresh basil leaves, torn into bite-sized pieces

1/3 cup olive oil

2 tablespoons balsamic vinegar

Salt

Pepper

Cube the fresh mozzarella, chop the tomatoes, into bite-sized pieces, and finely chop the basil leaves. Toss all together with oil, vinegar, salt, and pepper and serve immediately.

An alternative to the Chopped Caprese Salad, is to make a Layered Caprese Salad. Use a shallow glass dish to layer slices of mozzarella, tomatoes, and basil leaves. Stand the slices on end so that they are perpendicular to the dish. Alternate slices of mozzarella and tomato, making sure to place a leaf of basil between each slice. After all has been layered, sprinkle with coarse sea salt and coarsely ground black pepper. Drizzle vinegar over the top of the layers followed by a drizzle of olive oil. Serve immediately.

NUTRITION FACTS 6 servings. Per serving: Calories: 257.1; Fat: 21.6 grams; Protein 10.3 grams; Carbohydrate 2.8 grams; Fiber 0.4 grams

Mom's White Cole Slaw

My mother made Cole slaw this way as long as I can remember except she used sugar. Swapping the sugar for an approved sweetener was an easy way to still enjoy this family favorite. The poppy seeds are an optional addition, but add a really nice flavor and texture to this slaw.

INGREDIENTS

3/4 cup mayonnaise

2 1/2 tablespoons apple cider vinegar

1/4 teaspoon salt

1/4 teaspoon fresh cracked black pepper

1/4 cup sweetener, powdered OR 6 drops liquid sweetener

1/2 teaspoon poppy seeds

4 cups cabbage, shredded

Whisk together first 6 ingredients and pour over cabbage. Mix well. Let sit in the refrigerator for at least 30 minutes before serving. Adjust sweetener to your taste. This recipe is made to serve a crowd. You can easily cut it in half if you're feeding fewer people.

NUTRITION FACTS 16 servings. Per serving: Calories: 56.9; Fat: 6.9 grams; Protein 0.5 grams; Carbohydrate 2.6 grams; Fiber 1.1 grams

Red Cole Slaw

Red slaw is one of those regional North Carolina BBQ favorites. In the east, they tend to serve white slaw and in the western part of the state, red slaw. I always thought I preferred white slaw until I made red slaw. This stuff is good! Red slaw is especially good with pulled pork. Use my homemade ketchup on page 108 for the ketchup used in this recipe.

INGREDIENTS

1/2 cup homemade or low sugar ketchup
1/3 cup apple cider vinegar
1/4 teaspoon salt
1/4 teaspoon fresh cracked black pepper

1/4 cup sweetener, powdered OR 7 drops liquid sweetener
1/8 teaspoon cayenne pepper or dash hot sauce (optional)
4 cups cabbage, shredded

Whisk together first 6 ingredients. Pour over the shredded cabbage and mix well. Adjust sweetener to your taste. Let sit in the refrigerator for at least 30 minutes before serving.

NUTRITION FACTS 16 servings. Per serving: Calories: 5.5; Fat: 0 grams; Protein 0.5 grams; Carbohydrate 2.5 grams; Fiber 1 grams

Cauliflower Pizza Casserole

This side dish will quickly take center stage on your dinner table! I tend to serve it with simple meat dishes since this casserole has a lot of flavor.

Video: http://bit.ly/CookingKetoWithKrisiteCauliflowerRecipes

INGREDIENTS

Filling

3 cups cauliflower, cooked and pureed
3 ounces pepperoni, chopped
1 cup mozzarella, grated
1/3 cup fresh parmesan, grated
1 tablespoon sundried tomato, finely chopped (optional)
1 teaspoon Italian seasoning
1/4 teaspoon garlic powder
1/4 teaspoon onion powder

Topping

1 ounce pepperoni slices
4 ounces cooked sausage (optional)
3 ounces black olives, drained and sliced (optional)
1/2 cup mozzarella

Mix the cooked cauliflower puree, chopped pepperoni, cheeses, and seasonings in a large bowl. Pour the mixture into a greased glass baking dish. Top with whole pieces of pepperoni and desired toppings. Sprinkle 1/2 cup shredded mozzarella over the top. Bake at 350 degrees for 18 to 22 minutes until browned and bubbly.

NUTRITION FACTS 6 servings. Per serving: Calories: 308; Fat: 24.9 grams; Protein 14.9 grams; Carbohydrate 3.6 grams; Fiber 1.3 grams

Chapter 4

SASSY SAUCES & DRESSY DRESSINGS

Most cookbooks of this size would not have such a big section of sauces, dressings, or condiments; however, when you cook low carb high fat, these recipes become important. First, sauces are a great way to add additional fat and flavor to your low carb meals. Many have butter or cream as a base, creating a rich high fat meal that keeps you satisfied and not deprived. There's an avocado crema and a salsa Verde to add to your favorite Mexican dishes and a Thai Peanut Sauce and Asian Ginger dressing for an Asian flavor. Both are great served over salads or with meats like chicken or beef. The tzatziki recipe is a traditional Greek cucumber sauce that goes great with lamb, beef, or chicken.

Second, I included recipes for salad dressings because many commercial brands are primarily canola oil or soybean oil. These types of oils are thought to be inflammatory and to contribute to cardiovascular disease. I avoid them as much as possible. Besides, once you make these low carb options, you will likely prefer homemade salad dressings. The flavor is just much better than what you can buy. In addition to the two Asian dressings, I've included traditional ranch, blue cheese, and honey mustard dressing as well as a very basic vinaigrette.

Last, this section also has recipes for ketchup and a traditional BBQ sauce as well as a white BBQ sauce popular in the South. While I never imagined that I would make my own ketchup, we now prefer it because it simply tastes better. Moreover, I've found that making my own ketchup is far less expensive than buying the low carb versions that use questionable ingredients. The ketchup keeps for at least two weeks in the refrigerator and serves a base for the traditional BBQ sauce that has bacon fat as one of the secret ingredients. The white BBQ sauce is mayonnaise based, and we have not found a tastier way to add fat to low fat meats like white meat chicken. Both the ketchup and the BBQ sauce can be used in other recipes such as Rueben casserole or BBQ chicken fathead pizza. This diet is delicious!

Kristie's Ketchup

Yes, I know there are "low carb" commercial ketchups, and I used to use them, but when I started paying attention to quality ingredients, then I decided to try making my own. Not only is making your ketchup far less expensive, but it truly tastes better. This ketchup recipe is also the base for the Better Keto BBQ sauce, so I often make two batches and turn the second batch into BBQ sauce.

Video: http://bit.ly/CookingKetoWithKristieKetchupandBBQSauce

INGREDIENTS

8 ounces tomato sauce

2 tablespoons apple cider vinegar

1/3 cup Sukrin gold (brown sugar sub) OR 1/3 cup of your preferred granulated sweetener

1/8 teaspoon cinnamon

1/8 teaspoon cloves

1 teaspoon garlic powder

1 teaspoon onion powder

Mix all of the ingredients together in a small sauce pan. Simmer for 10 to 15 minutes on low heat to thicken. Store in the refrigerator for up to 2 weeks.

NUTRITION FACTS
16 servings. Per serving: Calories: 5.5; Fat: 0 grams; Protein 0.3 grams; Carbohydrate 1.1 grams; Fiber 0.3 grams

Better Keto BBQ Sauce

If you're looking for a great versatile BBQ sauce to enjoy when grilling, this is it. The addition of the cloves and cinnamon is what really makes this BBQ sauce special, so don't skip those two spices. We use it on pulled pork, ribs, and wings. Be sure to make plenty for a dipping sauce for the table. Our non-low carb family members and friends always ask for the recipe and that's high praise!

Video: http://bit.ly/CookingKetoWithKristieKetchupandBBQSauce

INGREDIENTS

8 ounces tomato sauce (no sugar added)	1 teaspoon garlic powder
2 tablespoons apple cider vinegar	1 teaspoon onion powder
1 tablespoon prepared mustard	1/2 teaspoon salt
1 tablespoon Worcestershire sauce	Sweetener to taste
1/8 teaspoon ground cloves	1 tablespoon bacon fat
1/8 teaspoon cinnamon	1/4 teaspoon liquid smoke (optional)
1/2 teaspoon ground mustard	1/4 teaspoon cayenne (optional)

Melt bacon fat in a small saucepan, add tomato sauce, apple cider vinegar, and Worcestershire sauce and heat to a low simmer. Simmer for 4-5 minutes before adding the remaining ingredients. Simmer on low heat for an additional 10 to 15 minutes to allow the sauce to thicken. This sauce keeps well in the refrigerator for at least 2 weeks.

NUTRITION FACTS 16 servings. Per serving: Calories: 13.5; Fat: 0.8 grams; Protein 0.3 grams; Carbohydrate 1.2 grams; Fiber 0.3 grams

White BBQ Sauce {Bama Sauce}

White BBQ Sauce is favored in some regions of the South. I didn't grow up with it, so I'm making up for lost time. This is one of my absolute favorite low carb sauces. Use a good mayonnaise that is free of sugars and preferably made with good oils, and you will see what I mean. White BBQ is more a table sauce than a cooking sauce and is especially good with roasted or smoked chicken, but is also tasty with pulled pork, brisket, grilled pork chops, or roasted turkey. Come to think of it, I haven't found anything it isn't good with!

INGREDIENTS

1 1/2 cup mayonnaise
5 tablespoons white wine vinegar
1 clove garlic, minced
1 teaspoon black pepper
2 teaspoon spicy mustard

1 teaspoon granulated sweetener or 1 drop liquid sweetener
1 teaspoon salt
2 teaspoons prepared horseradish

Use a whisk to mix all ingredients.
Store in a glass jar in the refrigerator.
Will keep for up to two weeks.

NUTRITION FACTS 16 servings. Per serving:
Calories: 114.5; Fat: 13.6 grams; Protein 0.1 grams;
Carbohydrate 0.4 grams; Fiber 0 grams

Blue Cheese Dressing

This dressing is tangy and rich. You can adjust the amount of blue cheese to your taste, but this is a simple, classic flavor. Use over salads or as a dip for chicken wings, pork rinds, meats, and veggies.

INGREDIENTS

1/3 cup mayonnaise

1/4 cup sour cream

3 teaspoons lemon juice or 2 teaspoons white vinegar

1/4 teaspoon garlic powder

1/4 teaspoon salt

1/4 cup heavy cream

4 ounces blue cheese crumbles

Use a whisk to mix mayonnaise, sour cream, lemon juice, garlic, salt, and cream. When well blended, add in blue cheese crumbles and mix well. Allow to chill for about 45 minutes before serving.

NUTRITION FACTS 6 servings. Per serving: Calories: 169; Fat: 15.7 grams; Protein 4.3 grams; Carbohydrate 0.8 grams; Fiber 0 grams

Photo courtesy of Debbie Roach

"Honey" Mustard Vinaigrette

Honey Mustard has always been one of my favorite dipping sauces, and this low carb version is no exception. When I make a batch for salads, it often ends up on meats or vegetables or as a dip for pork rinds instead. When I actually make a salad, I really enjoy this over spinach served with grilled chicken or salmon.

INGREDIENTS

3 tablespoons Dijon mustard
1/4 cup apple cider vinegar
1/4 teaspoon salt
1/3 cup avocado oil
1/4 teaspoon garlic powder

6 drops liquid sweetener (to taste)
1/4 teaspoon cayenne pepper (optional)
1 tablespoon mayonnaise (optional for creamy dressing)

Mix all ingredients in a small blender, shake in a mason jar, or whisk with a wire whisk. Blending this dressing will help to incorporate the fats. Adding mayonnaise will give the dressing a more creamy texture. Store in the refrigerator for up to two weeks.

NUTRITION FACTS 8 servings. Per serving: Calories: 82.7; Fat: 1.1 grams; Protein 0 grams; Carbohydrate 0.2 grams; Fiber 0 grams

Simple Vinaigrette Dressing

Bottled salad dressings are convenient, but it is often difficult to find one that doesn't have inflammatory oils or added sugars. The most basic salad dressing you can make is a simple oil and vinegar. Using different oils can change the flavor of the salad dressing. My husband doesn't care for the taste of olive oil, so we sometimes use avocado oil, walnut oil, or even hazelnut oil. For the vinegar, plain white vinegar has the most neutral flavor, followed by white wine vinegar, and then apple cider vinegar which has the strongest flavor. Adding mayonnaise or sour cream is optional, but adds a creamy option to this recipe. Experiment with your own oils and vinegars or keep it simple as I have in this basic vinaigrette recipe.

INGREDIENTS

1/3 cup olive oil or avocado oil

1/4 cup vinegar (white wine or apple cider)

1/2 teaspoon garlic, minced

1/2 teaspoon Italian seasoning

1/8 teaspoon salt

2 tablespoons mayonnaise or sour cream (optional)

Use a whisk to combine all ingredients, or seal the ingredients in a glass jar and shake well. Without the mayonnaise or sour cream, this does not need to be refrigerated, so it travels well.

For a creamy salad dressing option add 2 tablespoons of mayonnaise or sour cream or 1 tablespoon of each.

NUTRITION FACTS 6 servings. Per serving: Calories: 106.7; Fat: 12.5 grams; Protein 0 grams; Carbohydrate 0.2 grams; Fiber 0 grams

Asian Ginger Dressing

Sweet and tangy, this dressing mimics the dressings often served at Asian restaurants. Fresh, minced ginger works best in this recipe. Adjust the sweetness to your preference and serve as a salad dressing or use it as a sauce for meats. This is a very good sauce for chicken wings.

INGREDIENTS

1 teaspoon fresh garlic, minced

1 1/2 tablespoons fresh ginger, minced

1/4 cup coconut aminos (or soy sauce)

3 tablespoons rice vinegar (no sugar added) or white vinegar

1 tablespoon sesame oil

1/3 cup olive oil (or avocado oil)

8 drops liquid sweetener or 1/4 cup Sukrin Gold fiber syrup

Mix all ingredients in a mason jar and shake well. Alternately, you can mix with a whisk or blender. The dressing may need to be mixed again before serving or after being refrigerated.

NUTRITION FACTS 6 servings. Per serving: Calories: 137.3; Fat: 14.8 grams; Protein 0 grams; Carbohydrate 1.1 grams; Fiber 0 grams

Photo courtesy of Debbie Roach

Creamy Béchamel Sauce

Some of my tastiest recipes are created while I'm busy making other recipes. I made this sauce for the White Chicken Lasagna recipe, and then decided that it deserves its own billing. Béchamel is a considered a "mother sauce". Made with flour and milk, it is an excellent base for cheese sauces and other savory sauces. I used a combination of ingredients to mimic traditional Béchamel. Professional chefs might reject my efforts, but this is an excellent keto approximation. This is divinely rich and increases the fat profile of lower fat meats such as white meat chicken and of vegetables. If you adore Brussels sprouts or asparagus, this sauce is a perfect way to fatten those and to create an impressive side dish for guests. I look forward to hearing the creative ways that you use this recipe!

Video: http://bit.ly/CookingKetoWithKristieWhiteSauce

INGREDIENTS

4 ounces cream cheese	1/4 teaspoon salt
3 tablespoons butter	1/2 cup heavy cream
1 cup bone broth	3 teaspoons Worcestershire sauce
1 teaspoon dried parsley	1/2 cup sour cream
1 teaspoon garlic	1/4 teaspoon glucomannan

In a heavy saucepan, use medium to low heat to melt the butter and cream cheese with the bone broth. Stir or whisk frequently. When melted, add parsley, garlic, Worcestershire sauce, and salt. Whisk at low heat until the mixture simmers. Whisk in sour cream and heavy cream. Keep the heat low so that the sauce doesn't break. Whisk until the sauce is smooth and creamy. Add the glucomannan by sprinkling it over the sauce while stirring so that it doesn't clump. Glucomannan will thicken the sauce as it cools.

NUTRITION FACTS 8 servings. Per serving: Calories: 160; Fat: 36.5 grams; Protein 2.5 grams; Carbohydrate 1.6 grams; Fiber 0 grams

Thai Peanut Sauce

Asian Peanut Sauce is super versatile. You can use it over a cold cabbage "salad" or incorporate it into a hot sautéed chicken dish served over Miracle noodles (glucomannan noodles). This sauce is even better a day or two after it's made and is a tasty option for easy summer salads.

Video: http://bit.ly/CookingKetoWithKristieAsianPeanutSauce

INGREDIENTS

13.5 ounce can of coconut milk

1/3 cup creamy peanut butter

1/2 cup coconut aminos or tamari

2 tablespoons rice wine vinegar

1 tablespoon sesame oil

1 tablespoon lime juice

1 tablespoon fresh ginger

1 tablespoon garlic

1 tablespoon fish sauce

4 drops liquid sweetener (optional)

1/4 teaspoon cayenne pepper

Add the peanut butter and coconut milk to a heavy sauce pan on medium heat. Stir or whisk until smooth and blended. Stir in the remaining ingredients. Lower the heat and keep stirring until all ingredients are warmed through. Do not simmer. Use as warm or cold as a sauce or dressing. Refrigerate leftovers. Will keep up to one week in the refrigerator.

NUTRITION FACTS
16 servings. Per serving: Calories: 57; Fat: 8.2 grams; Protein 1.8 grams; Carbohydrate 2.8 grams; Fiber 0.5 grams

Avocado Crema

If you think guacamole is good, wait until you meet its sophisticated cousin. Avocado crema brings a presence that plain guacamole doesn't. Like a classic set of pearls, this dish pairs with your best heels or your favorite blue jeans, which means you can serve it to company or use it for dipping pork rinds. I always serve it with my carnita recipe (page 70) and with carne asada (page 71).
Video: http://bit.ly/CookingKetoWithKrisiteAvocadaCrema

INGREDIENTS

1 cup avocado
1 bunch fresh cilantro, stems removed
1/3 medium sized onion
1 fresh jalapeno, seeded
1/3 cup sour cream or crème fraiche

1 tablespoon lime juice
1/4 teaspoon salt
1/2 teaspoon cumin
2 teaspoons garlic powder

Add all ingredients to a blender or food processor. Blend until smooth and creamy. You may want to add a tablespoon or two of water for a thinner consistency. Chill and serve garnished with fresh cilantro.

NUTRITION FACTS 6 servings. Per serving: Calories: 72; Fat: 5.8 grams; Protein 1 grams; Carbohydrate 4.1 grams; Fiber 1.8 grams

Salsa Verde

Sandy taught me to make Salsa Verde when we made Sandy's Picadillo (page 74). I adapted her version and wanted to share it as an excellent sauce for carnitas (page 70), Mexican Chorizo Frittata (page 25), or fajitas. It also makes a spicy dip for pork rinds or homemade cheese chips. If you like a very mild spice, be sure to remove the seeds and stem from the jalapeno before pureeing the sauce.

Video: http://bit.ly/CookingKetoWithKristiePicadillo

INGREDIENTS

1 quart water
8 tomatillos, husked
1/4 small onion
1 large jalapeno
1 clove garlic

2 tablespoons fresh cilantro
1/3 cup water
1 tablespoon lime juice
1/2 teaspoon salt

In a medium-sized pot, add the raw veggies and cover with the quart of water. Bring to a boil until the tomatillos and the jalapeno soften, about 10 to 15 minutes. The jalapeno will change to an army green color. Strain out the water and puree the vegetables in a blender or Ninja. Add 1/3 cup or so of water to thin the chile sauce and blend until smooth. For a creamy option, add 1/2 of an avocado just before pureeing the cooked vegetables.

NUTRITION FACTS 12 servings. Per serving: Calories: 10; Fat: 0.2 grams; Protein 0.2 grams; Carbohydrate 2 grams; Fiber 0.6 grams

Tzatziki Sauce

Tzatziki is a creamy, savory cucumber sauce often served with Greek dishes. Most frequently, I serve it with Greek meatballs (page 55), but it also makes an excellent accompaniment to Greek salads, grilled chicken, or grilled lamb. I simply adore the fresh taste of lemon, garlic, and cucumber in this sauce.

Video: http://bit.ly/CookingKetoWiithKrisiteTzatzikiSauce

INGREDIENTS

1 1/4 cup full fat sour cream or crème fraiche

1/2 cup finely chopped cucumber

1 teaspoon minced garlic

1 tablespoon lemon juice

1 teaspoon dehydrated onion or finely chopped red onion

3/4 teaspoon ground cumin

3/4 teaspoon dried dill

1/4 teaspoon salt

Grate or finely chop the cucumber. Drain on towels to remove moisture. Mix the cucumber and all remaining ingredients and refrigerate to let flavors blend. The flavors are best if allowed to chill for at least 30 before serving.

NUTRITION FACTS 6 servings. Per serving: Calories: 96.3; Fat: 8.4 grams; Protein 1.7 grams; Carbohydrate 2.7 grams; Fiber 0.1 grams

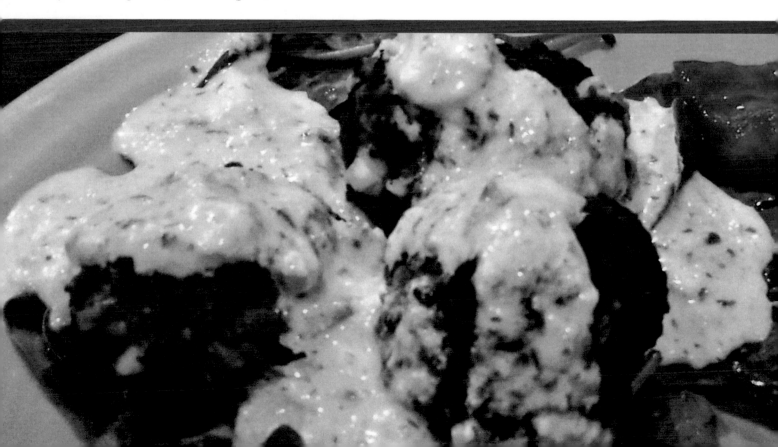

Grandmother's Hot Bacon Fat Vinaigrette

My grandmother used to make a hot bacon fat dressing that I adored. In my lifetime efforts to lose weight before keto, I embraced low-fat packaged dressings that quite honestly tasted like plastic. This, my friends, is how real dressing should taste. Serve it warm over a Spinach Salad (page 75).

Video: http://bit.ly/CookingKetoWithKristieBaconFatDressing

INGREDIENTS

1/2 cup of bacon fat
4 tablespoons of apple cider vinegar
1 tablespoon of Dijon mustard
salt

pepper
7 drops liquid or 3 tablespoons
granulated sweetener

Heat the bacon fat in a saucepan. Whisk in the vinegar, mustard, and other ingredients until it is well blended. Taste first for sweetness. I like a lot of ACV and a little more sweetener for extra tang.

NUTRITION FACTS 6 servings.
Per serving: Calories: 152; Fat: 16 grams;
Protein 0 grams; Carbohydrate 0 grams;
Fiber 0 grams

Classic Ranch Dressing

Classic Ranch Dressing can be made in two steps. The first part of the recipe calls for creating a dry mix that can be used in other recipes. The dry seasoning can be stored in the fridge or pantry, so that you can make ranch dressing quickly or you can use the dry mix to season other recipes. The second part of the recipe provides the wet ingredients you need to prepare the dressing. Just add two tablespoons of the dry mix to the wet ingredients to create a low carb version that is good with anything.

INGREDIENTS
Dry Mix
2 teaspoons black pepper
3/4 cup dried parsley flakes
1/3 cup garlic powder
1 1/2 tablespoon salt
1/3 cup onion powder
1 tablespoon dried dill weed

3/4 cup mayonnaise
3/4 cup heavy whipping cream
3/4 cup sour cream
1/2 teaspoon of lemon juice

Combine all dry ingredients and mix well. Store the mix in an airtight container in the refrigerator. Yields a little less than 2 cups of dry mix. For a fine powder to use with pork rinds or cheese chips, mix the dry ingredients in a blender.

Mix 2 tablespoons of dry mix with the mayonnaise, heavy cream, sour cream, and lemon juice. Let chill for at least two hours before serving. This recipe makes over two cups of dressing.

NUTRITION FACTS 16 servings. Per serving: Calories: 157; Fat: 16.1 grams; Protein 1.1 grams; Carbohydrate 2.2 grams; Fiber 0 grams

Thousand Island Dressing

Thousand Island dressing is probably one of the first salad dressings I liked, and I was probably drawn to it because it was so sweet. This low cab version uses my homemade ketchup (recipe page 108) and unsweetened pickle relish to lower the carb count. We mainly use it for the Rueben Casserole on page 60, but it is also delicious on a juicy bacon cheeseburger—hold the bun!

INGREDIENTS

1/2 cup mayonnaise

2 tablespoons homemade low carb ketchup

2 tablespoons low carb pickle relish

1/4 teaspoon garlic powder

2 teaspoons minced onion or 1/2 teaspoon onion powder

2 teaspoons vinegar

1/4 teaspoon salt

10 drops liquid sweetener (to taste)

Mix all ingredients and let chill for at least 30 minutes before serving. Keeps in the refrigerator for up to one week.

NUTRITION FACTS 6 servings. Per serving: Calories: 108.4; Fat: 12.8 grams; Protein 0 grams; Carbohydrate 0.5 grams; Fiber 0 grams

Photo courtesy of Sondy Murray

Chapter 5
FATHEAD
TO
FLATBREAD

While I have included some basic low carb bread recipes, I want to be frank about using them. Think of your favorite sandwich. While I no longer have a favorite sandwich in the traditional sense, I have always loved a good Philly cheesesteak. Consider what makes those so good. It's the steak—tender and fatty and that steak is topped with grilled peppers and onion that have been grilled in fat, preferably butter. On top of the steak, peppers, and onions is melted cheese—gooey and luscious. Add some mayonnaise, and there's not much more worth eating in the world. Notice what we didn't mention? The bun. The bread has no real flavor unless it's grilled and slathered with butter. The fat brings the flavor. Consider pasta and the same is true. The flavor and goodness of the dish is in the sauce. Alfredo anyone? Even pizza crust is just dry dough without fat in the form of cheese or oil.

Bread and pasta are really more of a habit, than a tasty food option. We can make a quick meal with a slice or two of bread or by easily boiling pasta. Both are also inexpensive. Together, the convenience and price, mean that bread and pasta are a staple of most households. Unfortunately, it is very high in carbohydrates and many argue that wheat is unhealthy for reasons that extend beyond carbohydrates. When folks switch to a low carb high fat way of eating, they often struggle with needing quick, easy, inexpensive meals. Many are accustomed to relying on bread or pasta for daily meals, so they look for good low carb alternatives not realizing that the flavor is in the filling.

Low carb bread substitutes are often disappointing for those just starting a low carb lifestyle. Even my favorite biscuit recipe included here is not "just like" your grandmother's biscuit. While Soul Bread is a great option for grilled sandwiches, it will not make a fluffy white bread tomato sandwich, and I will not lie about that because I am a Southern girl and that would be blasphemy.

I have included these basic "bread" recipes so that you will have these as options in your low carb lifestyle. If you use them, please be careful with the carbohydrate count. The Soul Bread is fantastic toasted and slathered with butter and even better used in a grilled sandwich fried up in a skillet. Like other low carb baked goods, it's better the day after you make it. You will also find two biscuit recipes. One is Belle's Biscuits and it is a favorite of my YouTube subscribers. It takes a LOT of egg whites. You can buy the egg white cartons or separate whole eggs and use those yummy yolks to make a batch of homemade low carb ice cream. The ice cream recipe is included in the Treats section of this book. The second biscuit recipe, Miracle Biscuits, are my favorite. They rise up and are the closest in flavor and texture of any low carb biscuit recipe I've tried. Just don't overmix them. The flatbread recipe is nut free and is so easy to make that my daughter made it by herself when she was 12. With olive oil, it reminds me of pita bread. We use it for school lunches and grilled sandwiches at home. The very best recipe in this section is truly the Fathead Pizza recipe. With the variations I've included, this is the closest to "real" pizza that you can make low carb. These crusts can be baked and frozen and used for quick meals that even the kids can make by themselves. Trust me when I tell you that even our carbivore friends and family enjoy the Fathead pizza.

Belle's Biscuits

When I was in college, I was nicknamed "Belle", as in Southern Belle. Along with a set of pearls, I had my signature biscuit recipe, Belle's biscuits. My friends would always ask me to make biscuits for them and any trip "home" with a friend usually resulted in a couple of batches of biscuits along with teaching the friend's mother how to make them. When we started eating low carb high fat, I feared my biscuit making days were over. As I discovered low carb high fat recipes and learned more about baking with alternative flours, I began tweaking recipes. This recipe is the result. In addition to using finely ground almond flour, I use oat fiber. Oat fiber has zero net carbs and gives low carb baked goods a more traditional flour-like mouth feel. It's a wonderful addition to any low carb pantry.

Video: http://bit.ly/CookingKetoWIthKristieBellesBiscuits

INGREDIENTS

10 egg whites

2 1/2 cups fine almond flour

4 tablespoons oat fiber (or 2 1/2 tablespoons coconut flour)

1/2 cup shredded mozzarella

2 teaspoons baking powder

1/2 teaspoon xanthan gum (can omit)

1 teaspoon salt

1 tablespoon erythritol (or your preferred sweetener)

6 tablespoons butter

Use a hand mixer to beat the egg whites until frothy, but not stiff. Add in almond flour, oat fiber, mozzarella cheese, baking powder, xanthan gum, salt, and erythritol and mix well with the hand mixer. Add in butter and beat with the hand mixer until well blended. Grease a muffin tin and fill each well 3/4 full. Bake at 400° for 10-12 minutes.

NUTRITION FACTS
12 servings. Per serving: Calories: 166.1; Fat: 19.7 grams; Protein 8.2 grams; Carbohydrate 2.9 grams; Fiber 1.5 grams

Red Lobster Imposter Biscuits

How can you make a biscuit better? Start with bacon, garlic, and cheddar. These savory biscuits are really good on their own, used for a low carb breakfast sandwich, or paired with a low carb soup.

INGREDIENTS

10 egg whites
2 1/2 cups fine almond flour
1/4 cup oat fiber (or 2 1/2 tablespoons coconut flour)
1/2 cup shredded mozzarella
2 teaspoons baking powder
1/2 teaspoon xanthan gum or glucomannan (optional)

1 teaspoon salt
1 teaspoon garlic powder
1 tablespoon granulated sweetener
6 tablespoons butter, melted (use 3 tablespoons bacon fat and 3 tablespoons butter if preferred)
1/3 cup bacon crumbles
1 cup shredded cheddar cheese

Use a hand mixer to beat egg whites until frothy, but not stiff. Add in almond flour, oat fiber, mozzerella cheese, baking powder, xanthan gum, salt, garlic powder, and erythritol and mix well with the hand mixer. Add in butter and use hand mixer until well blended. By hand fold in the cheddar cheese and bacon pieces. Grease a muffin tin and fill each well 3/4 full. Bake at 400° for 10-12 minutes. You may also bake them as drop biscuits on parchment paper on a baking sheet instead of using a muffin tin. This recipe makes 12 biscuits.

NUTRITION FACTS 12 servings. Per serving: Calories: 214.6; Fat: 23.3 grams; Protein 11.8 grams; Carbohydrate 3.2 grams; Fiber 1.5 grams

Photo courtesy of Sondy Murray

Miracle Biscuits

Miracle biscuits remind me of a traditional southern biscuit. There is only one egg in the entire recipe and each biscuit is roughly 1 carb. The oat fiber gives these a flour-like mouth feel. I named them Miracle Biscuits because the texture is so fantastic. Over mixing them makes them flat and tough. Use a gentle hand to mix and shape them. Grab some oat fiber, mozzarella cheese, and cream cheese and let's get to rolling in the dough!

Video: http://bit.ly/CookingKetoWithKristieMiracleBuscuits

INGREDIENTS

1/3 cup almond flour

1/3 cup plus 2 tablespoons oat fiber

1 tablespoon Sukrin: 1 granulated sweetener

1/2 teaspoon salt

1 teaspoon baking powder

1 egg

1 cup shredded mozzarella cheese

2 ounces cream cheese

3 tablespoons butter

Mix the dry ingredients and the egg and set aside. Melt the mozzarella cheese and cream cheese on reduced power in the microwave or melt together on low heat on the stove top. Warm until the cream cheese and mozzarella are well mixed. Add butter to the mixture to melt it. Add the warm cheese mixture to the dry mix and combine. You will need to use your hands to knead and combine the cheese and other ingredients. If the dough becomes stringy, warm it. Do not over mix the dough. Shape the dough into biscuits by hand. Be careful to handle them gently. Over mixing will makes the biscuits flat and tough. Place the biscuits on a baking sheet lined with parchment paper. Bake at 330 degrees for about 12 minutes. Biscuits will be lightly browned on top and bottom. The recipe makes 12 small biscuits or 10 medium-sized ones.

NUTRITION FACTS 12 servings.
Per serving: Calories: 85.3; Fat: 7.6 grams; Protein 3.3 grams; Carbohydrate 0.8 grams; Fiber 0.3 grams

Fathead Pizza Dough

This is my variation of the very popular fathead pizza dough. Using less almond flour and adding oat fiber lowers the overall carb count while keeping the wheat-crust mouth-feel we all enjoy. Even the carbivores will ask for this!

Video: http://bit.ly/CookingKetoWithKristieFatheadPizzaDough

INGREDIENTS

1 1/2 cups shredded mozzarella
2 tablespoons cream cheese
1/3 cup almond flour
1/3 cup oat fiber

1 egg
1 teaspoon garlic salt
1 teaspoon Italian seasoning

Melt the cream cheese and mozzarella on medium heat on the stovetop or in the microwave. Mix well. Add the almond flour and oat fiber and incorporate into the melted cheese. It's easiest to do this by hand with well-oiled hands. If the "dough" becomes stringy, warm it again. Last, add the egg and seasonings and mix well.

Line a baking sheet or pizza stone with parchment paper. Use your hands to flatten the dough or put a second piece of parchment paper on top of the dough and flatten it. Bake the flattened dough at 350 degrees for 10 to 12 minutes or until browned. When browned, add a few tablespoons of tomato sauce. Be sure to get a brand with no sugar added and use sparingly to minimize carbs. Top with your favorite low carb toppings such as pepperoni, cooked sausage, bacon, or olives and cheese. Return to the oven and bake until the cheese is melted and bubbling. You can also make the crusts ahead of time and then pull them from the fridge or freezer. If you don't have oat fiber, use 1/2 cup of almond flour.

NUTRITION FACTS 6 servings. Per serving: Calories: 152; Fat: 12 grams; Protein 8.7 grams; Carbohydrate 1.8 grams; Fiber 0.67 grams

{ *nut free* }

Basic Flatbread

Flatbread is really good with cold salads or when used for grilled sandwiches. This recipe uses coconut flour and psyllium husk powder to make a sturdy flatbread that is very low carb. Using olive oil gives this flatbread a taste that resembles pita bread. The cheese can also be omitted to make this recipe dairy-free.
Video: http://bit.ly/CookingKetoWithKristieFlatbread

INGREDIENTS

1/2 cup coconut flour
1 tablespoon psyllium fiber
1/4 cup olive oil
1 cup boiling water

1/3 cup parmesan cheese (or mozzarella)*
1/4 teaspoon sea salt
1/4 teaspoon granulated garlic
3/4 teaspoon Italian seasoning herb blend

Whisk all of the dry ingredients together in a mixing bowl. Add the olive oil and cheese. Add the hot water last, stirring as you add it. The psyllium will absorb the water, but be sure to keep mixing and to mix well so that it doesn't clump.

Flatten the dough onto unbleached parchment paper-lined jelly roll pan until thin and even. I line the pan with

Photo courtesy of Sondy Murray

parchment paper and then place a second piece of parchment paper on top and use my hands to flatten and smooth the dough. Be sure that it is a uniform thickness. You should have enough dough that, when flattened, it will cover a 9' by 13" jelly roll pan.

Bake at 350° for 20 to 25 minutes. The baking time will depend on how thin you've rolled the bread. When browned, transfer to a cooling rack, peel away the parchment paper and allow to cool to room temperature. I use a pizza cutter to cut it into squares for sandwiches.

NUTRITION FACTS 8 servings.
Per serving: Calories: 50;
Fat: 2.4 grams; Protein 2.8 grams;
Carbohydrate 4.5 grams;
Fiber 2.5 grams

Modified Soul Bread with Oat Fiber

The original recipe for Soul Bread was developed by Gloria Koch (Soul's Song). Her recipe is very good, but I decided to modify it using oat fiber, bacon fat, apple cider vinegar, and yeast. The yeast provides flavor, but does not contribute to the rise. The texture is coarse and improves after the bread is completely cooled. When toasted and buttered, it is really very good. Thanks to Soul Bread, grilled cheese sandwiches can be part of a low carb lifestyle.

Video: http://bit.ly/CookingKetoWithKristieSoulBread

INGREDIENTS
12 ounces of cream cheese, softened in the microwave
4 eggs
1/4 cup heavy cream
1/4 cup melted butter
1/4 cup bacon fat melted
2 tablespoons apple cider vinegar

Dry Ingredients
1 1/4 cup whey protein isolate (Isopure or Hoosier is recommended)
1/2 cup oat fiber
1/4 teaspoon salt
1 package yeast (for taste)
1/4 teaspoon baking soda
1 teaspoon xanthan gum
2 1/2 teaspoons baking powder
1/4 teaspoon cream of tartar

Use a hand mixer to blend the cream cheese, eggs, cream, butter, bacon fat, and apple cider vinegar. Mix well and set aside. Mix dry ingredients in a separate bowl. Use a whisk to thoroughly mix the dry ingredients. Next, use a sieve or sifter to sift dry ingredients into the wet ingredients. Stir in in lightly. Do not overmix. Add 4 drops of liquid sweetener if you'd like.

Preheat the oven to 325 degrees. Pour the dough into two 8.5" by 4.5" bread pans greased liberally. Bake for 45 minutes until golden brown. A toothpick can help test for doneness in the middle. Don't under bake or the bread will sink as it cools. Let cool at least 15 to 20 minutes before slicing. The flavor and texture of this bread improves the day after it is made. I enjoy it best used as a grilled sandwich or toasted in a toaster and slathered with butter.

NUTRITION FACTS
16 servings. Per serving: Calories: 383.9; Fat: 6.9 grams; Protein 9.7 grams; Carbohydrate 0.7 grams; Fiber 0.2 grams

Chapter 6
TREATS

Among the low carb high fat community there seems to be two schools of thought. The first oppose using treats of any kind, especially when beginning a low carb high fat diet. The second school of thought embraces treats as a way to transition from a traditional diet with desserts and goodies. Among the objections by those who eschew treats are the concerns that these types of foods might delay the healing process, including weight loss. Also, they fear that having treats with low carb sweeteners might perpetuate or feed cravings and that by avoiding low carb treats they will no longer crave the high carb counterparts. In addition, they choose to avoid treats to give their taste buds time to adapt to foods and flavors without sweeteners. In the other camp, are those who enjoy low carb fat bombs, minute muffins, cheesecakes, pies, cookies, and cakes. The general thought is that you can enjoy a low carb dessert in moderation and still make your way to better health. For some of these folks, choosing a low carb cookie is a much better option than diving face first into a box of Oreos. Having treats helps to make the "diet" feel more normal and can also help during holidays or celebrations when you can join friends and family socially, not feel deprived, and stay on plan.

Many people have asked me which is "best", to have treats or to avoid them? In general I respond by asking which is better, driving a Toyota or a Honda? Well, it depends. Both will likely get you where you want to go. What matters is the trip. Is the seat comfortable? Can you reach the gas pedals? Can you afford the insurance, gas, and maintenance? Is there room for your family and your things? Remember that this trip is about the journey, not the destination. You have to determine whether you want the scenic route or the interstate. Sometimes the "best" route is a combination of both, but what is most important is staying on the route. If eating a low carb treat might throw you off course or tempt you with a pattern of bingeing, than definitely avoid them. On the other hand, if having a low carb birthday cake is important to you, then it's very good to have options so that you don't feel deprived and end up with hydrogenated vegetable shortening icing on the tip of your nose!

While I understand and respect both sides of the argument, I tend to fall on the side of enjoying low carb treats in moderation. I've shared my story of the peanut butter cookie that saved my life. Near the end of my first two weeks of going low carb high fat I had a terrible craving for a cookie. I imagined myself getting in the car, driving to the store, buying a pack of Pepperidge Farms soft baked chocolate chip cookies, and stuffing my mouth full. Instead, I muttered "Just for today, just for today!" all the way home from my office. When I got home, I looked up low carb cookie recipes. The only one that I had the ingredients for was a peanut butter cookie. It had only 4 ingredients: peanut butter, egg, sweetener, and baking powder. As I made the cookies, I worried that it might not be a good idea or that it would stall me. Desperate, I made them anyway, promising that I would not eat more than two cookies. I took the first bite. That cookie was so good, and I thought, "If I can eat foods like this and still lose weight, I can do this for the rest of my life." And I have.

The treats I've included here are some basic fat bombs, which are a way of adding higher fat to our day without adding protein or carbs. Also, fat bombs are an excellent way to fight cravings. They are difficult to overeat because they make us feel full. Besides fat bombs, I've included a very basic cheesecake recipe that even novice cooks can easily make. If you're worried about portion control, I've added a single serving chocolate minute muffin that will satisfy your sweet tooth and keep you on plan. The other treats are also pretty simple and are the favorites of my family like Key Lime Pie that I make for my husband or peanut butter cups which I have to hide from all of us. Of course, I had to include the Peanut Butter Hero Cookie recipe that saved my life during those first two weeks when I was adapting to a low carb high fat lifestyle. Just in case you're celebrating a birthday, there are three cake recipes included here. One is a basic pound cake that can be made into a round layer cake. The second is a peanut butter cake, and the third is a basic chocolate cake recipe that is really delicious with a peanut butter buttercream. What goes better with cake than ice cream? You don't have to miss that either. I've included two delicious ice cream flavors—mint chocolate chip, which is my daughter's favorite flavor, and Cookie Dough, which I make at David's request. Last, there is also a nonsweet "treat" here and that is a No Chex Mix made with a combination of pork rinds and nuts. I consider it a treat because the nuts make it higher carb, and I make it mostly during the holidays since the high carb version has always been a family favorite during the holidays. With so many fantastic low carb dessert options, why would we ever eat any other way?

Not "Chex" Mix

Chex mix was always on my grandmother's side table during the holidays, and it became a tradition at my house as well. My brother especially enjoyed it, so it became my tradition to make a batch just for him. When we went low carb, I didn't want to make the high carb traditional version, so I started brainstorming substitutes. Not only does this work, but we think it works even better. The crunch is fantastic!
Video: http://bit.ly/CookingKetoWithKristieChexMix

INGREDIENTS

3 ounces fluffy pork rinds, broken into bite-sized pieces

3 ounces crunchy pork rinds, broken into bite-sized pieces

100 grams pecans pieces

100 grams peanuts

7-8 tablespoons unsalted butter, melted

2 tablespoons Worcestershire sauce

2 teaspoons seasoning salt

1 teaspoon garlic powder

1/2 teaspoon onion powder

Using different types of pork rinds: the crispy, thin cracklin', the "popcorn", and the fluffy pork rinds are a great way to vary the texture of this mix. You need about 4 or five cups all in small, bite-sized pieces. Throw those into a large bowl with the pecans and peanuts. In a separate glass bowl, melt the butter. Add Worcestershire sauce, garlic powder, and onion salt. Mix the spices into the melted butter and pour over the pork rind and pecan mixture. Mix well to coat. Spread on a baking sheet and bake at 300 degrees for about 30 minutes, stirring every 7-8 minutes. Let cool and enjoy!

*If you don't have different types of pork rinds, use what you have. I like to use only pecans and pork rinds to keep the carbs low, but you could add other nuts or other low carb kibbles.

NUTRITION FACTS
8 servings. Per serving: Calories: 381; Fat: 33.8 grams; Protein 17.1 grams; Carbohydrate 4.4 grams; Fiber 2.4 grams

Peanut Butter Hero Cookies

These are the cookies that saved my life! In the first two weeks of a ketogenic diet, I had a terrible craving. I made these cookies, took the first bite and thought, "If I can eat this and still lose weight, then I can do this for the rest of my life!" That was in June 2013, and I still plan to eat this way for the rest of my life.
Video: http://bit.ly/CookingKetoWithKrisitePBHeroCookies

INGREDIENTS

2 cups of creamy peanut butter

1 1/2 cups granulated sweetener (Sukrin Gold brown sugar sub)

1 teaspoon of baking powder

2 eggs

1/2 teaspoon salt

1 tablespoon vanilla extract

1/4 cup Sukrin Fiber Syrup Gold (optional but adds crisp to cookie)

Mix peanut butter and sweetener until smooth. Add the remaining ingredients and mix well. Roll into 1 inch diameter balls and press into cookies. You can drag a fork across the top to make a crisscross pattern. Bake at 350 degrees for 9 to 10 minutes. Cookies will be chewy when first out of the oven. Let cool on a baking rack to let cookies become crisp. Store in the refrigerator.

NUTRITION FACTS 48 servings. Per serving: Calories: 69.9; Fat: xx grams; Protein 5.5 grams; Carbohydrate 2.4 grams; Fiber 1 grams

Never Fail Cheesecake

Cheesecake is pretty easy to make low carb if you can figure out the crust and substitute for the sugar. My version isn't fussy and always has a winning texture with the full-fat dairy I use. For the crust, you can lower the carb count by 1 carb per serving by using hazelnut flour instead of almond flour. Chocolate ganache poured over the top makes this simple recipe a special occasion dessert.

Video: http://bit.ly/CookingKetoWithKristieCheesecake

INGREDIENTS

Crust
3/4 cup almond flour
1/3 cup granulated sweetener (Sukrin :1)
1/3 cup oat fiber (optional)
3 1/2 tablespoons butter, melted
1/4 teaspoon vanilla extract
Dash salt

Filling
24 ounces cream cheese, softened to room temperature
1/2 cup granulated sweetener (Sukrin :1)
1/3 cup heavy cream
3 eggs
4 drops liquid sweetener
2 teaspoons vanilla extract
1 teaspoon lemon juice

Mix all of the ingredients for the crust. Press the crust into the bottom of a springform pan. Set aside. Use a hand mixer to whip the cream cheese until smooth. Add the granulated sweetener and mix until blended. Add the eggs, one at a time, beating well after each. Add the heavy cream and continue to mix the batter until smooth. Add the liquid sweetener, vanilla extract, and lemon juice. Pour the batter over the prepared crust, smoothing the top to be even. Bake at 350 degrees for 40 to 45 minutes or until set. Let cool and refrigerate at least 6 hours before cutting. Overnight is best. If you don't have a springform pan, use a 9" by 13" glass baking dish or a large pie pan.

NUTRITION FACTS 12 servings. Per serving: Calories: 341; Fat: 33.7 grams; Protein 7.2 grams; Carbohydrate 4 grams; Fiber 0.8 grams

Photo courtesy of Jen Reitz Scholz

Perfect Pound Cake

While we like to joke about it, I believe that it was my traditional pound cake recipe that really won my husband's heart. My pound cake was legendary! It has taken a lot of tries, but this low carb pound cake is as close to perfect as I have been able to create. I can't promise it will win you a proposal, but it's worth a try if you find someone worth the trouble.

INGREDIENTS

1/3 cup coconut flour

1/4 cup of oat fiber

1 teaspoon baking powder

1/2 teaspoon salt

4 ounces unsalted butter, softened

1/2 cup granulated sweetener (Sukrin :1)

5 large eggs

1/2 cup heavy cream

2 teaspoon vanilla extract

4 or 5 drops of liquid sweetener

Mix the dry ingredients well with a wire whisk and set aside. In a mixing bowl, use a hand mixer to whip the butter and granulated sweetener. Add eggs, beating well after each addition. Stir in heavy cream and vanilla extract by hand. Add dry ingredients and mix in by hand, being careful to not over stir. Add liquid sweetener to taste. Pour batter into a well-greased loaf pan and bake at 350 degrees for about 20 to 25 minutes. You can also use one 9 inch round cake pan and bake for 16-20 minutes. Test for doneness by touch or when a toothpick inserted in the center comes out clean.

NUTRITION FACTS 12 servings. Per serving: Calories: 147.3; Fat: 13.5 grams; Protein 3.3 grams; Carbohydrate 2.4 grams; Fiber 1.1 grams

Kristie's Favorite Granola Nut Bars

If you used to love granola bars, these are completely addictive. Before you object, I have used a combination of ingredients to lower the carb count as much as possible. My picky husband does not like pork rinds and does not like coconut flakes. He never knew either ingredient was in there! Please trust me on this. Everyone who has ever tired this has been shocked when (if) they found out there were pork rinds in them. Just be sure to use the big, fluffy pork rinds that have a very mild flavor. Carolina Country Cracklins, Larry's Pork Rinds, and Brimm's are three of my favorite brands.

INGREDIENTS

1/3 cup macadamia nuts, chopped

1/2 cup pecans, chopped

1/3 cup almonds, chopped

2 tablespoons butter

1 tablespoon coconut oil

2 tablespoons coconut flakes, fine macaroon unsweetened

2 tablespoons hemp seeds

2 tablespoons sunflower seeds

1/2 cup chopped pork rinds

1 scoop vanilla whey protein isolate

1/3 cup Sukrin Gold Fiber Syrup (or 8 drops liquid sweetener)

1/4 teaspoon cinnamon

1/8 teaspoon salt

In a large skillet, mix chopped macadamia nuts, pecans, and almonds. Add 2 tablespoons of melted butter and stir on low heat until nuts are browned. Add coconut oil and remove from heat. Stir in coconut flakes, hemp seeds, sunflower seeds, and pork rinds and mix well. Add whey protein isolate and stir to coat mixture. Add Sukrin Gold Fiber Syrup or liquid sweetener and mix well. Please note that while the liquid sweetener will add sweetness, the Sukrin Fiber Syrup helps to make the nut bars chewy. If the mixture is dry, add more butter or coconut oil. Pour the mixture into a greased 9" by 13" glass dish and smooth until flat. The back of a wooden spoon works well to evenly distribute the mixture. Let cool for at about 45 minutes before slicing into bars.

NUTRITION FACTS 12 servings. Per serving: Calories: 226.3; Fat: 20.2 grams; Protein 6.9 grams;

Carbohydrate 4.4 grams; Fiber 2.3 grams

Grace's Granola

Grace didn't develop this recipe, but she did help me develop it. She is my chief taste tester, and if G says yes, then I can count on that recipe to make others smile.

INGREDIENTS

3 cups pork rind pieces

1 cup raw pecan pieces

1/3 cup raw pumpkin seeds

1/2 cup raw sunflower seeds

4 ounces butter

4 ounces coconut oil

2 tablespoons cinnamon

1/3 cup granulated sweetener (Sukrin :1)

10 drops liquid sucralose

1/3 cup unflavored or vanilla whey protein isolate

Break the pork rinds into small bits. I used a mix of fat back rinds and fluffy skins for texture. Heat oven to 250 degrees. In a large bowl, mix pork rinds, pecan pieces, pumpkin seeds, and sunflower seeds. Set aside. The seeds can be omitted to lower the carb count, but are nice for texture.

In a saucepan on low heat, melt the butter with coconut oil. Add cinnamon, sweetener, and liquid sucralose. Add the whey protein isolate. When the mixture is melted and mixed well, pour it over the pork rinds, pecans, and seeds. Mix well until all is covered with the wet mixture. Spread it onto a parchment or foil covered baking dish and bake at 250° for about 30 minutes. Turn off the oven, and leave the oven door open. Let the granola sit in the oven for at least an hour and a half with the oven light on. The longer you leave it, the crunchier the granola becomes. Store in an airtight container.

NUTRITION FACTS 8 servings. Per serving: Calories: 641; Fat: 60 grams; Protein 28.4 grams; Carbohydrate 6.25 grams; Fiber 3.375 grams

Low Carb Peanut Butter Cups

Those darn Chocolate Peanut Butter Easter Eggs mock me, and this recipe lets me mock them right back! I can have my chocolate covered peanut butter treats AND stay on plan. These are a favorite in my house and a great help to the Easter bunny. Adding peanut flour gives these peanut butter cups a more authentic taste and texture. Be sure to buy peanut flour with just ground peanuts and nothing added. Sukrin makes a great peanut butter flour.

Video: http://bit.ly/CookingKetoWithKristiePBCups

INGREDIENTS
2 3-ounce low carb chocolate bars
2 teaspoons coconut oil

Peanut Butter Filling
8 ounces peanut butter
1/2 cup powdered sweetener (Sukrin Melis)
1 teaspoon pure vanilla extract
1/16 teaspoon of cinnamon
1/4 cup peanut butter flour (optional, but gives a great texture)

Mix 8 ounces of peanut butter with extract, cinnamon, peanut flour, and powdered sweetener. Set aside. Melt the chocolate on a very low heat. Add coconut oil to the chocolate and stir constantly with a small whisk. Heat on low heat and heat just until melted and smooth.

Line a mini-muffin pan with paper or foil muffin liners. Use a small spoon to coat the mini-muffin liners with chocolate. See the video link if you need clarification. Shape the peanut butter filling into a flat disc about 1 inch in diameter. Put the small disk of peanut butter on top of the chocolate in each liner, and then cover that with more of the melted chocolate. Do not be tempted use a lot of chocolate in each as you just want a thin coating. This recipe makes 36 mini peanut butter cups.

NUTRITION FACTS 36 servings. Per serving: Calories: 72; Fat: 6.5 grams; Protein 2.3 grams; Carbohydrate 1.9 grams; Fiber 1 grams

Chocolate Mint Fat Bombs

Fat bombs rescue me. They rescue me from cravings and from missed meals because I'm on the go. You can omit the coconut butter from this if you don't have it. The fat bombs will not be as thick, but they will be equally delicious. I store mine in the freezer, so they are always handy when I need one.
Video: http://bit.ly/CookingKetoWithKristieFatBombs

INGREDIENTS

4 ounces coconut oil

4 ounces butter

2 tablespoons coconut butter or coconut manna

3 drops peppermint oil

3 tablespoons cocoa powder

1/4 teaspoon instant coffee

1/4 teaspoon cinnamon

1/2 teaspoon vanilla

1/4 teaspoon salt (omit if using salted butter)

1/3 cup powdered sweetener (Sukrin Melis)

3 drops liquid

Melt the coconut oil and butter in a sauce pan on low heat. Add coconut butter, cocoa powder, coffee, cinnamon, and salt. Stir well. Add sweeteners and peppermint oil. Taste for sweetness and adjust as needed. Let the mixture cool to room temperature and then blend it in a mixer or use an immersion blender to mix it very well so that it doesn't separate while setting up. Pour into candy molds or into an 9" by 9" glass dish. Refrigerate immediately and let set for at least two hours. If the mixture separates, you likely needed to blend it after it had cooled more. If that happens, melt it, cool to room temperature, and blend again.

NUTRITION FACTS 12 servings. Per serving: Calories: 116; Fat: 13 grams; Protein 0.8 grams; Carbohydrate 0.7 grams; Fiber 0.3 grams

Peanut Butter Fat Bombs

By the tablespoon, peanut butter is a carb bomb. At seven carbs per tablespoon, it's a meal's worth of carbs for me. One way around that is to make fat bombs that "cut" the carbs with pure fat. This recipe does just that and has less than 1 total carb per serving. I keep these in the freezer and use them if a meal hasn't been satisfying, as a meal replacement, or to battle cravings when they sneak in.

Video: http://bit.ly/CookingKetoWithKristieFatBombs

INGREDIENTS

4 ounces of butter

4 ounces of coconut oil

2 tablespoons of peanut butter

1/2 teaspoon vanilla extract

1/4 teaspoon cinnamon

1/4 teaspoon salt, if using unsalted butter or unsalted peanut butter

1/3 cup powdered sweetener (Sukrin Melis) or liquid sweetener to taste

In a saucepan, melt the butter, coconut oil, and peanut butter. Stir until smooth. Add the vanilla, cinnamon, salt, and sweetener. Remove from heat and blend in a mixer or use an immersion blender to mix. Refrigerate immediately. Be sure to mix it very well so that it doesn't separate while setting up.

NUTRITION FACTS 12 servings. Per serving: Calories: 161; Fat: 18 grams; Protein 0.7 grams; Carbohydrate 0.6 grams; Fiber 0.3 grams

Pumpkin Spice Fudge

Pumpkin Spice Fudge is a tasty fall treat that you can easily make year round for anytime you need a taste of fall. You can adjust the spices to your preference. I tend to like milder spices to let the pumpkin flavor shine. You can add more pumpkin if you prefer, but the fudge will have a softer texture and there will be more carbs per serving.

Video: http://bit.ly/CookingKetoWithKristieFatBombs

INGREDIENTS

6 ounces coconut oil

4 ounces butter, salted (ghee for dairy free)

1/2 cup pumpkin puree

1/3 cup Sukrin Melis, powdered sweetener

1 teaspoon vanilla extract

1/2 teaspoon maple extract (optional)

1 teaspoon pumpkin pie spice

1/2 teaspoon cinnamon

1/4 teaspoon ground cloves (optional)

Melt the coconut oil and butter in a heavy saucepan on low heat. Stir in the pumpkin and powdered sweetener. Remove from heat and stir in the extracts and spices. As the mixture cools to room temperature use an immersion blender or hand mixer to blend it really, really well. If the mixture isn't cool enough, the fudge will separate when it cools in the fridge. Pour the mixture into an 8" by 8" glass dish. Refrigerate immediately and let set for at least 2 hours or until firm. Cut into squares and store in the fridge or freezer.

NUTRITION FACTS 12 servings. Per serving: Calories: 127; Fat: 21.7 grams; Protein 0.7 grams; Carbohydrate 0.9 grams; Fiber 0.3 grams

Mocha Fluff

Mascarpone cheese and crème fraiche are rich and creamy treasures that are full of fat and intensely satisfying. I use crème fraiche instead of sour cream as frequently as I can because of the higher fat. In this recipe, I combine cocoa powder and coffee to turn these two favorites into a quick and simple delightful treat!

INGREDIENTS

8 ounces mascarpone cheese (may sub cream cheese)

8 ounces crème fraiche (may sub sour cream)

1 teaspoon vanilla extract

2 teaspoons instant coffee granules

2 tablespoons cocoa powder

3 tablespoons warm water

1/8 teaspoon salt

12 drops liquid sweetener

Mix mascarpone and crème fraiche by hand and set aside. In a separate small bowl, mix coffee granules and cocoa powder. Add warm water and stir until well dissolved. Add chocolate and coffee mixture to the mascarpone and crème fraiche mixture. Add salt, sweetener, and vanilla. Mix lightly until thoroughly blended. Let chill for at least 30 minutes before serving.

NUTRITION FACTS 4 servings. Per serving: Calories: 450; Fat: 110 grams; Protein 4.8 grams; Carbohydrate 2.3 grams; Fiber 0.5 grams

Chocolate Minute Muffins

Minute muffins are ideal for a number of reasons. First, because it is a single serving, you automatically have portion control. In addition, they are quick. We mix up the dry ingredients in advance, and then add the wet ingredients whenever we want chocolate cake. Last, these really do taste like a treat, but they make a great breakfast. In fact, I love eating them for breakfast at work or when I'm in hotels because they travel well. Last, who doesn't love chocolate cake for breakfast?

INGREDIENTS

2 tablespoons almond flour

1 teaspoon oat fiber (or add an additional teaspoon of coconut flour)

1/2 teaspoon baking powder

1 tablespoon cocoa powder, unsweetened

1 teaspoon coconut flour

1 tablespoon granulated sweetener (Sukrin :1)

1/8 teaspoon instant coffee (optional)

1 egg

2 tablespoons butter, melted

2 drops liquid sweetener

1/4 teaspoon vanilla extract

1 ounce low carb chocolate, chopped (optional)

Mix dry ingredients with a whisk. Add melted butter, egg, and vanilla extract and mix until smooth. Add liquid sweetener and chopped chocolate if using. Taste for sweetness. Divide mixture and pour into two well-greased ramekins or coffee mugs. Microwave for 1 minute. Muffins should firm up and dry out as they cool. A dollop of whipped cream makes this muffin extra special.

NUTRITION FACTS 2 servings. Per serving: Calories: 195; Fat: 18 grams; Protein 5 grams; Carbohydrate 3.7 grams; Fiber 1.8 grams

Peanut Butter Chocolate Chip Bundt Cake

Peanut butter cake, chocolate chips, peanut butter buttercream, and chocolate sauce form alternating layers of two classic flavors in a humble Bundt cake. This, my friends, is church homecoming worthy.

INGREDIENTS

1/2 cup peanut flour
1/3 cup almond flour
1/3 cup protein powder
1/3 cup oat fiber
2 teaspoons baking powder
3/4 teaspoon salt
8 ounces butter, softened
1 cup sweetener (Sukrin :1)

4 drops liquid sweetener
4 ounces cream cheese
4 ounces peanut butter
4 eggs, room temp
1 tablespoon vanilla extract
3 ounces chopped low carb chocolate
(optional)

Use a whisk to blend together flours, baking powder and salt. Set aside. In a mixing bowl, use a hand mixer to whip the butter and to blend in sweetener. Once the butter lightens in color, it is well mixed. If the butter becomes grainy-looking, it is too warm. Add cream cheese and peanut butter and mix until smooth. Add eggs, beating well after each. Add vanilla extract and mix well. Add the dry ingredients to the large mixing bowl, stirring in by hand. Add chopped chocolate or chocolate chips if desired.

Bake in a well-greased medium sized Bundt pan or a 9" by 13" glass pan or bake in a muffin tin at 350 degrees. This batter will need to bake in a Bundt pan for 35 to 45 minutes. Test for doneness by touch or when a toothpick inserted in the center comes out clean. Top with Peanut Butter Buttercream on page 147 and/or Chocolate Drizzle.

NUTRITION FACTS 16 servings. Per serving: Calories: 272.8; Fat: 23.6 grams; Protein 11.6 grams; Carbohydrate 3.9 grams; Fiber 1.6 grams

Peanut Butter Buttercream Icing

Peanut Butter Buttercream—just the name is creamy and dreamy. This buttercream is great on my low carb chocolate cake or the peanut butter chocolate chip Bundt cake, and even more heavenly if you add a chocolate glaze or chocolate chips. Peanut Butter Buttercream is also great served on the end of a spoon.
Video: http://bit.ly/CookingKetoWithKristiePeanutButterButterCreamIcing

INGREDIENTS

8 ounces salted butter, softened
1 cup powdered sweetener (Sukrin Melis)
10 ounces creamy, salted peanut butter

1 teaspoon vanilla extract
3 to 4 drops liquid sweetener

Use a hand mixer to blend the softened butter and powdered sweetener. When the butter and sweetener are creamy, add the peanut butter and mix well. Add vanilla and liquid sweetener.

NUTRITION FACTS 12 servings.
Per serving: Calories: 214.2; Fat: 22 grams;
Protein 3.3 grams;
Carbohydrate 2.4 grams; Fiber 1.3 grams

Private Island Key Lime Pie

So many special things about this pie make it hard to describe. The macadamia nut crust really brings out the best of the island flavor, and while the filling sounds fussy, it is easy enough for Mr. Keto to make on his own. When you're zesting the limes, be sure to get only the flavorful green outermost part of the lime. If you get any of the white peel, it will be bitter. This pie is best enjoyed wearing flip flops and a tan, but I wouldn't turn it down even if I was in a blizzard!

INGREDIENTS

Crust

8 tablespoons butter, softened
1/2 cup granulated sweetener (Sukrin :1)
1/2 cup crushed macadamia nuts
1/2 cup almond flour
1/3 cup oat fiber
1 teaspoon vanilla extract

Filling

1/2 cup butter
1/2 cup powdered sweetener (Sukrin Melis)
1/2 cup key lime juice
1/4 cup lime zest
6 egg yolks
1 1/2 cups heavy cream
1/4 teaspoon glucomannan or xanthan gum
1 teaspoon vanilla extract
4 drops liquid sweetener

Mix all of the ingredients for the crust until a dough forms. A food processor works well, but you can also mix it by hand. Press the crust into a 9 inch glass pie pan. Be sure to press the crust up the sides. Bake the crust at 350 degrees for 12 to 14 minutes until just lightly browned. Set aside to cool. In a heavy saucepan, melt the butter on low heat. Whisk in the sweetener, lime juice, and zest. When the sugar is dissolved, whisk in egg yolks. Keep heat low and whisk constantly until the mixture starts to thicken. When it is thick, remove from heat and strain the mixture to remove the lime zest and refrigerate. In a large bowl, whip the heavy cream. As it begins to thicken, add the glucomannan, extract, and sweetener. Gently fold the whipped cream mixture into the chilled lime mixture. Mix lightly so that it remains fluffy. Use a spatula to fill the crust with the pie filling and to smooth it edge to edge. Let chill for at least an hour before serving. Garnish with lime slices, lime zest, or additional whipped cream.

NUTRITION FACTS 12 servings. Per serving: Calories: 396.5; Fat: 41.8 grams; Protein 3.8 grams; Carbohydrate 4.4 grams; Fiber 1.6 grams

No-Tella Chocolate Hazelnut Muffins

My family was previously addicted to the popular, sugar-filled chocolate hazelnut spread, and they still enjoy the flavors of chocolate and hazelnut. These muffins are moist and fluffy and only 2.5 carbs each since hazelnuts are lower in carbs than almonds. For that reason, I like to use hazelnut flour with a mix of almond flour in cheesecake crusts and other desserts. Hazelnuts have a more coarse texture and make a great low carb breakfast "bread".

INGREDIENTS

1 2/3 cup hazelnut flour
1/2 cup + 1 tablespoon cocoa powder
1/3 cup oat fiber
1 1/2 teaspoon baking powder
1/2 teaspoon salt
1 teaspoon instant coffee powder
4 ounces butter, softened

2 ounces cream cheese, softened
3/4 cup granulated sweetener (Sukrin :1)
1/3 cup hazelnut oil
3 eggs
8 drops liquid sweetener
1 teaspoon hazelnut extract
1 teaspoon vanilla extract
1/4 cup heavy cream

Mix first six ingredients, using a whisk to make sure it is well mixed. In a mixing bowl, cream together butter, cream cheese, and sweetener. Beat in the eggs, hazelnut oil, liquid sweetener, and extracts. Add the dry ingredients to the wet ingredients and blend well by hand adding heavy cream as you add the dry ingredients. Divide the muffin batter among 12 wells in a well-greased or paper-lined muffin tin. Bake at 350 degrees for 12 to 16 minutes. Muffins are done when they yield to a light touch or when a toothpick inserted in the center comes out clean.

NUTRITION FACTS 12 servings. Per serving: Calories: 208; Fat: 21.2 grams; Protein 3.2 grams; Carbohydrate 2.5 grams; Fiber 1 grams

Mint Chocolate Chip Ice Cream

Mint Chocolate Chip is a favorite of mine because the cold chocolate is crisp, but when it melts in your mouth it's creamy and then the mint flavor provides another blast of cool and crisp.   It also happens to be Grace's favorite flavor too, so I have a great excuse to make it.

Video: http://bit.ly/CookingKetoWithKristieIceCream

INGREDIENTS

2 1/4 cups heavy cream
5 egg yolks, beaten well
3/4 cups powdered sweetener (Sukrin Melis)
2 teaspoons pure vanilla extract

1/2 teaspoon salt
1.5 ounces finely chopped dark chocolate
2 drops food grade peppermint oil

In a heavy sauce pan, heat the heavy cream on low heat, stirring with a wire whisk. Add the egg yolks that have been beaten until barely frothy. Continue whisking on low heat until just warmed. Powder the sweetener in a blender or Ninja. Add to the cream mixture and whisk until well dissolved. Add vanilla, peppermint oil, and salt. Remove from heat and let cool in the fridge.   Follow the manufacturer's directions for making ice cream in your ice cream maker. Add the chopped chocolate pieces to the ice cream while it is still churning and after it has begun to freeze, but while the ice cream is still soft. Let the ice cream continue in the ice cream maker until it is ready to serve.

NUTRITION FACTS 6 servings. Per serving: Calories: 384.2; Fat: 37.8 grams; Protein 6.1 grams; Carbohydrate 3 grams; Fiber 0.5 grams

Chocolate Chip Keto Dough Ice Cream

Even without the chocolate chip cookie dough, this vanilla custard is the best ice cream I have ever eaten, sugar free or not. This is the ice cream that is "worth the trouble" of being homemade. Deceptively delicious and simple, this is how real ice cream should taste.

Video: http://bit.ly/CookingKetoWithKristieIceCream

INGREDIENTS

1/4 recipe low carb chocolate chip cookies, unbaked (recipe on page 154)

2 1/4 cups heavy cream

5 egg yolks, beaten well

3/4 cups powdered sweetener, powdered (Sukrin melis)

2 1/2 teaspoons pure vanilla extract

1/2 teaspoon salt

In a heavy sauce pan, heat the heavy cream on low heat, stirring with a wire whisk. Add the egg yolks that have been beaten until barely frothy. Continue whisking on low heat until just warmed. Powder the sweetener in a blender or Ninja. Add to the cream mixture and whisk until well dissolved. Add vanilla and salt. Remove from heat and let cool in the fridge. While the ice cream mixture cools, make a batch of low carb chocolate chip cookies. Divide the dough into four parts. Crumble 1/4 of the dough into small pieces. The pieces should be the size of small pebbles. Set aside. Follow the manufacturer's directions for making ice cream in your ice cream maker. Add the cookie dough bits to the ice cream mixture while it is still churning. Be sure that the ice cream has begun to freeze, but add the cookie dough while the ice cream is still soft. Let the ice cream continue in the ice cream maker until it is ready to serve.

NUTRITION FACTS 6 servings. Per serving: Calories: 432.5; Fat: 42.9 grams; Protein 6.8 grams; Carbohydrate 3.6 grams; Fiber 0.8 grams

Kristie's Carrot Cake Cheesecake

Carrot Cake Cheesecake is the very first low carb dessert recipe I created on my own. I was still learning how to use alternative flours, but I had gotten enough experience to feel mildly comfortable adding a little of this and a little of that. I had also figured out that cheesecake was a good low carb option and that it can be used to "stretch" the flavors of a higher carb favorite. Like a firstborn child, I'm proud of this recipe. Not only is it reliably good, but it gave me the confidence to keep creating.

Video: http://bit.ly/CookingKetoWithKristieCarrotCakeCheesecake

INGREDIENTS

Cake Batter

2 cups almond flour
6 tablespoons whey protein isolate
3 eggs
2/3 cup melted coconut oil or butter
1/2 cup heavy cream
1 1/2 cup granulated sweetener
(Sukrin :1)

2 teaspoon vanilla extract
1 teaspoon cinnamon
1/4 teaspoon salt
1/2 teaspoon baking soda
3/4 teaspoon baking powder
1 teaspoon apple cider vinegar
1/2 cup finely shredded carrots
1/2 cup walnuts (optional)

Preheat the oven to 300 degrees. Grease a 9" spring form pan with butter or coconut oil.

Mix melted coconut oil (or butter) with sweetener and extract. Add eggs, beating well. In a second bowl, mix almond flour, baking soda, baking powder, protein isolate, cinnamon, and salt. Combine well. Add flour mixture to egg mixture. Add cream and apple cider vinegar. Mix well. Stir in carrots and walnuts. The batter will be thick. Pour the batter into the greased spring form pan. Use the back of a spoon to push batter against the sides of the pan, creating a well for the cheesecake batter. Set aside and prepare the cheesecake filling.

INGREDIENTS

Cheesecake Filling

16 ounces full fat cream cheese

2 eggs

1/2 cup sweetener (Sukrin :1)

4 drops liquid sweetener

1 tablespoon vanilla extract

Mix the cream cheese, eggs, sweetener, and extract with a hand mixer. Pour the cheesecake batter on top of the cake batter, carefully adding a little batter at a time. Spoon the filling around the center and out to the sides up to 1/2 inch from the sides of the pan. Bake at 300 degrees for 50 to 55 minutes or until cake edges are browned and cheesecake center is set. Allow to cool for at least 6 hours or over night.

INGREDIENTS

Icing

8 ounces full fat cream cheese

4 tablespoons butter

1/4 cup powdered sweetener (Sukrin Melis) or liquid sweetener

1/2 teaspoon vanilla extract

Beat well with a hand mixer and spread over the cheesecake after it has completely cooled.

NUTRITION FACTS 16 servings. Per serving: Calories: 300.9; Fat: 28.6 grams; Protein 9.3 grams; Carbohydrate 4.1 grams; Fiber 1.8 grams

Keto Chocolate Chip Cookies

A diet without Chocolate Chip Cookies is just a diet. A diet WITH Chocolate Chip Cookies is a lifestyle. Most low carb cookies are soft and more cake-like in texture. It is difficult to achieve a crisp cookie and even more difficult to achieve a chewy cookie without sugar. If you can use Sukrin Fiber Syrup Gold, then this cookie will have a slightly chewier texture when it cools. Like most low carb baked goods, these are better when cooled and even more fabulous the following day.

INGREDIENTS

1 cup almond flour
3 tablespoons oat fiber (or 2 tablespoons coconut flour)
1/4 teaspoon baking soda
1/4 tsp cream of tartar
1/4 tsp xanthan gum (optional)
1/4 cup Sukin Gold brown sugar sub
1/4 cup granulated sweetener (Sukrin :1)

5 tablespoons melted butter
1 large egg
1 teaspoon vanilla extract
2 tablespoons Sukrin Gold Fiber Syrup. (optional, adds chewy texture)
3 tablespoons low carb chocolate chips (optional)
2 tablespoons chopped pecans (optional)

Note: If you don't have Sukrin products, use 1/2 cup of your preferred granulated sweetener.
Mix the dry ingredients. Set aside. Mix the wet ingredients. Combine the wet ingredients with the dry ingredients. Mix in low carb chocolate chips or chopped low carb chocolate. Add chopped pecans if desired. Mix until the ingredients form a thick dough. Shape the dough into a log and refrigerate for at least 3 hours. Slice into 12 slices and bake on parchment paper on a baking sheet at 350 degrees for 8 to 12 minutes. Let the cookies cool and then transfer them to a cooling rack. Cookies will firm up as they cool.
*Note. I always double the recipe. Also, the baked cookies freeze well. The cookie dough also freezes well.

NUTRITION FACTS 12 servings. Per serving: Calories: 177; Fat: 18.3 grams; Protein 3 grams; Carbohydrate 2.6 grams; Fiber 1.4 grams

ADDITIONAL RESOURCES FOR A LOW CARBOHYDRATE OR KETOGENIC LIFESTYLE

Fortunately there are several fantastic resources online that can either help you learn more about this way of eating or learn how to cook wonderful low carb foods. Whether you want to find recipes, review sample eating plans, learn more about the science, or hear from real people who have had success, there are some reliable resources. As always, when looking at recipes from others, please calculate the nutritional information for the ingredients you use. While I really appreciate and respect each of the food bloggers I've listed, some eat higher carb than I am able. Always use your best judgement as to what works well for you. Here are just a few of my favorites in each of those categories.

Information for beginners:

Diet Doctor was founded by Andreas Einfeldt, a physician in Sweden. He and his team provide a practical, no nonsense approach to a low carbohydrate diet. They accept no ads or sponsors, so the information they provide tends to be neutral and reliable. While much of the content is free, they do have a subscription-based service for additional information for a nominal monthly fee.
http://www.dietdoctor.com

Reliable science-based information:

These websites are either hosted by medical professionals or provide interviews and podcasts with medical professionals. You may find that they contradict each other at time, but that tends to simply highlight the areas that need more research.

Nusi, a non-profit dedicated to independent research. While NuSi was founded by Gary Taubes and Peter Attia, Dr. Attia is no longer affiliated with NuSi.
http://www.nusi.org

Zoe Harcombe is a researcher, author, blogger, and public speaker. She's one sharp cookie, and was among the first to examine the research base against dietary fat. If Dr. Harcombe says it, I believe her!
http://www.zoeharcombe.com

Mark Sisson is more of a paleo, primal, low carb advocate and focuses on eating whole, real foods and overall health. His website is entertaining and informative and covers a wide range of topics.
http://marksdailyapple.com

Dr. William Davis is a cardiologist who advocates a grain-free low carb lifestyle. While his blog has become more commercialized over the past year or so, there is still some useful information. His blog is easy to understand and he provides good basic information for people new to this lifestyle.
http://www.wheatbelly.com

The Poor, Misunderstood Calorie is a blog authored by Bill Lagakos, a Ph.D. in Nutritional Biochemistry and Physiology. His blog focuses in obesity, inflammation, and insulin resistance.
http://www.caloriesproper.com

Steve Cooksey used a low carb diet to manage diabetes after a health crises. He now focuses on a primal low carb approach.
http://www.diabetes-warrior.net

Dr. Jason Fung is a nephrologist in Canada. Dr. Fung has used a very low carb diet to treat diabetic patients with kidney disease. His writing style is entertaining and informative.
http://www.intensivedietarymanagement.com

Christine Cronau is a nutritionist who discovered low carb high fat in her 40s and used it to reverse debilitating health issues.
http://www.christinecronau.com

Professor Noakes' banting website has some very good information for folks new to low carb high fat. Some of the information is fee-based, but much of it is still available for free.
http://www.realmealrevolution.com

Dr. Eades maintains his blog Protein Power. A physician who uses a low carb diet to treat patients, his blog is very informative with practical advice and easy to read posts.
http://www.proteinpower.com/drmike/

Brian Williamson is the mastermind behind The Ketovangelist website. He has excellent podcasts and a very good blog with solid, practical support.
http://ketovangelist.com

Jimmy Moore's popular podcasts host a wide variety of guests, many of whom provide varying viewpoints.
http://livinlavidalowcarb.com

Hyperlipid is a blog authored by UK veterinarian Petro Dobromylskyj. While his blog is not an easy, casual read, it provides a thought-provoking and heavily science-based conversation about metabolism.
http://high-fat-nutrition.blogspot.com/

Optimizing Nutrition is a blog maintained by Marty Kendall. His blog focuses on the nutritional impact of foods and macronutrients. While the content is fairly advanced, he writes in such a way to make the information easy to understand.
http://optimizingnutrition.com

Favorite Low Carb Food Bloggers:
I am indebted to many of these talented and creative bloggers who not only provided delicious low carb recipes for my journey, but through their efforts I learned how create my own low carb recipes.

All Day I Dream About Food
If anyone can make a low carb dessert, it's Carolyn Ketchum. She's an incredible talent in the kitchen. Following her and making many of her recipes taught me a lot about baking for keto.
www.alldayidreamaboutfood.com

I Breathe, I'm Hungry
Melissa Sevigny is another creative genius. She has excellent dessert recipes, but she also has delicious main and side dishes. Check out her meatball Monday selections. You will not be disappointed.
www.ibreatheimhungry.com

Satisfying Eats
If Melissa at Satisfying Eats makes it, then you know it's really good. She's a Southerner too and her dishes never disappoint. She also offers some diary-free and nut-free alternatives.
www.satisfyingeats.com

Ruled Me
Craig has been blogging quite a while. He offers meal plans and recipes along with good information for beginners.
www.ruledme.com

24-7 Low Carb Diner
Lots of quick meals including crockpot and freezer meals at 24-7 Low Carb Diner.
www.247lowcarbdiner.com

DJ Foodie
While some of his recipes are higher carb than I can eat in a single meal, DJ Foodie is a culinary genius. His blog, and his cookbook, are excellent. I've relied on his recipes more than once.
www.djfoodie.com

Low Carb Maven
Kim is not only amazing in the kitchen, but her photography is exceptional. Be sure to pay attention to carbs and portions, but whether you're looking for dinner ideas or an impressive low carb dessert, she always has excellent ideas.
www.lowcarbmaven.com

She Calls Me Hobbit
Scott or the "hobbit" is simply one of the nicest fellas you could ever meet online, and he's a darn good cook to boot. He encouraged me more than once to put my own cookbook together, and I'm mostly grateful for that encouragement.
www.shecallsmehobbit.com

Maria Emmerich
Maria and her husband Craig adopted two of the cutest little boys ever. They are her "test kitchen", and are two very lucky fellas. Her recipes are reliable and delicious. She has a best selling cookbook that I don't have, but about which I have heard rave reviews.
http://mariamindbodyhealth.com/

Peace, Love, and Low Carb
Kyndra has great recipes. She has had a very public battle with regaining weight lost and has recommitted to her goals. Her story is reaching a lot of people.
http://peaceloveandlowcarb.com/

ABOUT THE AUTHOR

Kristie Sullivan lives in the beautiful Sandhills of North Carolina with her fantastic, handsome, patient, and nurturing husband, David aka Mr. Keto; their sweet, smart, generous, and cheeky daughter Grace; and their creative, curious, smart, and funny son, Jonathan. Two furry fellas are also an important part of their family. Banjo, a morkie (Maltese and Yorkie mix) is a 10lb killer, and Winston, an English Springer Spaniel, is a 70lb lap dog.

A born and bred Southerner, Kristie grew up in a small community called Big Lick, North Carolina. Raised in rural NC with very close extended family, she was fortunate to grow up in the some of the best kitchens of the South. Her grandmothers taught her early on that "ain't no recipe gonna show me how to cook". Their creativity, culinary instincts, and delicious meals, are the only training she has in the kitchen.

She earned her Ph.D. in Educational Research and Policy Analysis in 2010 from North Carolina State University. She began following a ketogenic diet in June 2013. While she adores her family from top to bottom, her life's passion has become helping others learn more about a ketogenic way of eating.

You can learn more about Kristie and follow her latest updates at www.cookingketowithkristie.com. You can also follow her Facebook page, Simply Keto and subscribe to her YouTube channel, Cooking Keto with Kristie.

42926004R10091

Made in the USA
Middletown, DE
26 April 2017